SURVIVING THE WITNESS BOX

Expert Opinion in Court

By
Dr. Phil Watts

Ogilvie Publishing

Copyright

© Dr Philip Watts, 2009 / 2021

Watts, Phil, 1962- .

Surviving the witness box: expert opinion in court / Author: Phil Watts

Ogilvie Publishing

PO Box 393

South Perth, 6951

Western Australia

Bibliography. Includes index.
ISBN 09756042 0 1 / 9780975604229

1. Evidence, Expert - Australia. 2. Witnesses - Australia.
3. Examination of witnesses - Australia. 4. Mental health personnel - Legal status, laws, etc. - Australia. I. Title.

Dewey Number: 347.94067

Editing and Indexing: Linda McNamara, South Perth
Printing: Lightning Source Australia

Acknowledgements

I would like to acknowledge the many readers of the 2004 edition of "A reliable witness" who provided positive feedback and encouragement. I hope you find this new book even more useful than the original edition.

While the original book was intended for the mental health profession, many non-psychologists have expressed an interest in the content. I especially thank David Burger, an electrical engineer, whose interest in my original book showed me that other professions have a need for a book about opinion evidence. As a result, this book has been written for broader audience.

I would like to give thanks to the many members of the legal profession who have taught me the art of appearing in court, including Kate Stockwell, Karen Farley, Donna Webb, Lucy Thomas, John Pacy, John Athanasiou, Julia Johnston, Sara Tovey and Frank Castiglione, to mention some of the notable influences. I also acknowledge the judges of the courts who through their judgments have increased my knowledge about the way in which evidence is perceived in court.

Two barristers, Steven Jones and David Childs, kindly provided constructive criticism of the original book and Robin Bourgeois has willingly reviewed this edition. I am deeply appreciative of their perspective as "insiders", which has added to my professional understanding.

The idea of developing a training seminar into print form came from Michael and Leslie Tunnecliffe. As a result of their original help I am now working on my fourth book. Their little seeds have germinated well. I thank them for their inspiration, encouragement and practical help, as I would never have considered taking on the task without it.

CONTENTS

1

The Nature of Court

Introduction

There are two types of witnesses in court. One may immediately think of those who survive and those who do not. That may indeed be the case but that is not the distinction to which I am referring. In considering the needs of the court there are witnesses of fact and witnesses of opinion.

A witness of fact is someone who gives evidence about what they have directly experienced via one of their five senses. In many ways this is the evidence preferred by the court. Unfortunately the situation is never that simple, and courts sometimes require professionals who can assist with things that are beyond the understanding of the average person (or the court). Therefore, experts who can offer an opinion are called to court to assist by providing specialist knowledge that they have accumulated from either study or life experiences or both. They are witnesses of opinion.

In the ever-increasing complexity of the world, courts need the assistance of professionals – experts who provide assistance across a wide range of subject areas. There are medical and health experts, including doctors, psychologists, physiotherapists and occupational therapists, who assist the court with health or injury evidence; accountants, who help with property disputes, financial issues, and evaluations; engineers or architects, who may give evidence about structural and design issues; environmental experts, who provide evidence on the impact of various processes on the environment, and so on. The court needs this help, so it turns to experts, both willing and reluctant, to assist in the legal process.

This book is intended to assist witnesses of opinion. While someone who is a witness of fact may find this book helpful, there are different issues applicable to the different types of witnesses. It is the professional person giving evidence I hope to assist.

When preparing this book, I was aware of the gap in the available Australian literature for the education of witnesses of opinion. Information provided by lawyers about giving evidence in court is available but it does not properly take into account the subtleties of individual professions. Such information is legally and technically correct but often tedious to read or irrelevant to non-legal professionals. This is particularly so because most non-lawyers do not understand the legal narrative. Academics have also written books which are extremely useful in a technical sense but, for the busy practitioner, seem dry and irrelevant.

I am an experienced forensic psychologist, which means that although I understand the mental health profession, I may not necessarily have a full understanding of the legal subtleties, nor the finer points, of other professions. I do, however, have extensive experience in giving evidence, and good evidence is good evidence irrespective of the profession involved. This book has been written to be a practical guide, rich with personal experience and useful advice. Therefore, I offer the following three cautions:

1. This book is designed to provide generic advice. It is important to realise that protocols vary between different courts, states and areas of law. If you appear in the Family Court, District Court, Supreme Court, or the Magistrates Court there are similarities and differences between the various courts. The better you understand the particular court environment, the better you will perform and the more credible you will appear. Please ensure that you seek local advice about the particular court to supplement the general details contained in this book.

2. I am not a lawyer and this book does not provide legal advice. What I offer are observations and experiences I have found useful in a court context. They are carefully considered but not infallible. If in doubt, seek legal advice before acting on the material in this book. Legal advice is relatively easy to obtain. The Yellow Pages and local law societies will readily refer you to lists of legal professionals willing to help. However, like the advice from any profession, make sure the person you deal with has the necessary competence and expertise in the particular area of law relevant to your issues.

3. Different professions have ethical standards that specify particular approaches to legal issues. For example, in the discussion on service provider issues in chapter two, I note that care should be taken to ensure that the boundaries between assessment/evaluation and treatment

or services are not blurred. This is consistent with the Australian Psychological Society's (APS) "Code of ethics" (APS 2007). The Royal Australian and New Zealand College of Psychiatrists (RANZCP) in their "Ethical and practice guidelines" #9 (RANZCP 2003) takes a firmer position by explicitly advising that psychiatrists should not provide routine treatment to patients referred for medical examinations except in exceptional circumstances. Whether you are an accountant, health professional, or engineer it is critical to ensure that you follow the ethical standards and codes of conduct relevant to your profession.

The Court Experience

Most professionals dislike court. This dislike varies from feelings of disdain, due to the disruption of their normal routines, through to absolute terror at the prospect of being examined critically in what is essentially an alien environment. The part of the legal process most professionals want to avoid is actually being in court and giving expert evidence. While often seen as an inconvenience, most people do not mind preparing material for court (normally some type of report).

What most professionals fail to adequately understand is that the credibility of the evidence is not just the result of how they appear in court on the day. While that is certainly a factor of great significance, much of the process is shaped by the position taken in the report they have already prepared. Likewise, the position taken in the report will be influenced by the way the professional deals with the initial contact from the lawyer. It is the position taken at the beginning that shapes how the report is written and how the evidence is given. This is the critical factor that will influence the sort of cross-examination you will receive at the trial.

This book is designed to be a practical guide to help explain to a professional each step of the legal process. The structure of the book loosely follows the process that results in an appearance in court. The second chapter examines ways in which you may get drawn into the court system and how this influences the structure of the report you provide. The third chapter examines some of the issues in relation to writing reports for court, as the report is the basis of the evidence to be given. The fourth chapter presents a model or mental map of how an expert needs to be perceived by the court. This is something that I have developed through my years of experience in court, and in my dealings with lawyers. Once mastered, you will never view court in the same way again and you will increase the likelihood of being perceived as a reliable witness. The fifth chapter looks at the skills required to be an effective witness, while the final chapter is a practical guide addressing some of the "how to" aspects of giving evidence in court.

The Fears

If you are reading this book, it is likely that you have some fears or anxieties about going to court, including being in a witness box (one of the major things people dread). There are five common causes for these fears.

In psychology we speak about the "ego", meaning the sense of our self. Court is threatening to the ego. An early experience in court, described below, is a good example of how an appearance in court made me feel inadequate. There are many different threats to the ego. It may be a fear of being "tricked" or of looking incompetent. Lawyers are good at making us feel bad so it is not an uncommon fear. There can also be the fear of how you perform, and even whether you will remember what you are supposed to say (going blank under pressure).

The fear of a loss of control is a problem in the court environment. Someone said that appearing in court is like duelling, except you have a very short sword! It is important to remember that you are not completely defenceless. Later in the book I will discuss how to make that short sword more effective. I would also point out that anxiety is linked with control; the less control you feel you have, the greater the anxiety. Therefore, regaining control is an essential anxiety management strategy.

There is a set of fears related to performance. This is the fear of going blank, saying the wrong thing or, in various other ways, failing to perform in the manner in which you think you should. This fear can never completely leave you, because it is linked to control. It is not possible to predict exactly what a lawyer is going to do. It is important to understand that the relationship of performance to anxiety is an inverted U shaped relationship. At low levels of anxiety you perform badly by being under prepared. If your anxiety levels are too high, then your performance is also going to be bad because you cannot think properly (as feelings increase, thinking decreases). Therefore you should aim for the optimum level of anxiety. Sports psychologists teach athletes how to manage anxiety by maintaining optimum arousal. If your arousal level is your problem (typically by being too high), you may need help to manage it better. It is a skill that can be learned with the aid of a competent psychologist.

When I run training courses on giving evidence in court, I discuss trauma as a common reason for the fear of going to court. If a person has had a previous bad experience, that person fears feeling like that again. Fear is normally adaptive. If a car nearly hits you, fear of walking on the edge of road keeps you safe. Unfortunately, as you are unable to get out of appearing in court, avoidance does not help. The opposite is the case; the fear gets worse when you do not get an opportunity to face it!

For many people who work in caring roles (such as doctors, psychologists and physiotherapists) going to court creates an empathy dilemma. We want the best outcome for our clients; we do not want them to have a bad outcome, so we get very protective of them.

When I first started to appear in court I thought that it was my job to have all the answers and to win the case. This was a mixture of my ego and an empathy dilemma. Now I have learned that I am one piece of the process and that my job is to present what I know to help the judge to make a decision. This makes the empathy dilemma easier.

In summary, court provokes anxiety. It is normal to experience great anxiety until you are familiar with the court environment; even an experienced witness will feel some arousal at the prospect of appearing in court. Court is an alien environment and lawyers want to keep it that way (so that they can have the longer sword in the "duel"). As your court skills develop these factors will be less of a problem for you. Therefore, if you understand the rules of the process, your performance will improve.

Key Points

- In court there are lay witnesses who only give evidence about the facts, and expert witnesses who offer professional opinions.

- The court needs evidence from expert witnesses who can offer an understanding greater than that of a "normal" person.

- The way in which opinion evidence is given in court will depend upon the rules of the court. These rules vary from state to state, and from court to court.

- An effective professional understands their professional and ethical obligations when working within the legal jurisdiction.

- The credibility of the evidence depends upon the way in which the professional initially establishes their role, and how they have structured the report upon which their evidence is based. It is not determined soley by the professional's performance in court (although that is important).

- There are five common fears associated with going to court. These fears include a fear of damage to the ego, loss of control, performance anxiety, re-traumatisation, and the empathy dilemma.

- Fears associated with appearing in court can be managed in the same way as any type of anxiety is managed. This includes improving your preparation, using anxiety management strategies, and understanding how the court process works.

- The goal is not to eliminate the anxiety but to keep it at an optimum level for peak court performance.

The Court "Game"

As you begin to deal with legal professionals (judges, barristers and lawyers), you will find yourself suddenly transported to another world. Within this alien world you will find that they use words of a familiar language in different ways, and also use terms from a different language. Things that are common sense and seem obvious are overlooked while, at other times, procedures become bogged down with strange rules and apparently petty details. Part of the message I hope to convey in this book is that the differences between the way in which your profession and the legal profession view situations can be understood. The book is designed to teach you about some of the subtle (and not so subtle) differences in communication and rules. In psychological jargon, lawyers use a different narrative (or story) in their communication processes with others.

Imagine yourself as a tourist visiting a new culture. You have to learn the language, customs and traditions of the local people if you are to survive in the new culture. So it is with court. I did not realise that I had to do this, so it was by chance rather than through any particular strategy that I started on the learning journey. The journey started when I was a new graduate, full of enthusiasm and naivety. In my first job I worked in a juvenile detention centre. One of my main tasks was to write reports for the Children's Court. After writing these reports they would be sent off in a manila envelope to an entity called the "court". Every now and then I was asked to go along and give evidence. When I had to appear in court it was terrifying. My early experience of appearing in court was that two seemingly very hostile people were trying to rip me to pieces while a stern looking judge alternated between frowning and looking bored throughout the process. At the end of it all, I would feel incredibly humiliated and would slink out of court, feeling lower than I ever thought possible. The experience terrified and humiliated me! I think it terrifies most other professionals too because in our own professional lives we are used to having our opinions and views respected and not critically challenged.

One day I was in the Children's Court and two lawyers

were having their usual go at me. The twist in this case was
that the lawyer who was cross-examining me happened to
be a new friend. Something about the court environment
had turned this normally compassionate friend into a
vicious assailant who was ripping me to pieces! When she
finished, the prosecutor, a police officer, also tried to rip
holes in my evidence. After they ended their attacks upon
me, and as the court adjourned for lunch, I tried to make
a hasty exit. My friend then approached me and asked:
"Phil, do you want to come to lunch?" As a result of my
recent experience I may have thought, "With you? Not in
this life!" Instead I politely smiled and said: "Oh sure, I
would love to." She then asked the prosecutor: "Do you
want to come too?"

Herein lies the apparent irony of the legal system. There
we were chatting together over lunch when moments
before we had been at each other in the most serious of
situations. That was when I realised that court is in some
ways like a game. It is a very serious "game" with big
decisions under consideration. It is very ego threatening
when you are not used to the rules, but it nonetheless
has some characteristics of a game. As a result of this
experience I began to try to understand not only how the
process works, but also its inherent rules. In my opinion,
it is just as critical to understand the rules as to produce
a good assessment (either clinically or using the tests
relevant to your profession). Prior to explaining the rules,
it is important to understand briefly why court systems
exist in every modern society.

Law and Government

Under the Australian Constitution there are three
separate streams of power. These are; the legislative power

(the Parliament), the executive power (constitutionally under the Governor-General), and the judicial power (the High Court and other federal courts). Most people in Australia know that the demarcation between the legislative and executive powers is somewhat blurred as the Governor-General rarely acts in an independent capacity (the functional executive is made up of ministers who are also members of the party, or coalition of parties, which holds a majority of seats in the House of Representatives). Therefore, although the Constitution clearly delineates three streams of power, the practical reality is that for most purposes there are only two separate streams; the government and the judiciary. As far as I am aware, most democratic societies have the law and government as separate entities. The purpose of having at least two streams of power is to ensure the good order of the country for the benefit of all people. The separation of law and government prevents the ruling body from enacting their own rules which are constitutionally inappropriate. Furthermore, individuals have rights but the government and law place limits on those rights for the good of the majority.

Sections 71-80 of the Australian Constitution provide for the creation of a High Court, and then specify the roles and powers of that body. In his book "How Australia is governed" (McNamara 1999, p.36) the author states: "The High Court is the supreme court of the country and its decisions must be accepted by everyone, including governments". It is quite profound to think that everyone, irrespective of what they may want or believe, must accept a decision. To cause all people to obey, the law has to consist of a set of rules powerful enough to ensure that this happens. A simple example is that requests for written or oral information by a court, called a subpoena, are very difficult not to comply with since the court needs information for the good of all people. A subpoena is backed up by large penalties for non-compliance to ensure that the court receives the information it needs when required.

One of the roles of the High Court is to interpret the laws enacted by Parliament. If someone does not like the way a law has been interpreted, an appeal may be lodged in a higher court. Eventually the High Court, as the highest court in Australia, may hear the appeal. Even appeals in relation to laws made by state governments may be heard by the High Court. Therefore, two types of law will be present in the system. There is the written law (legislation enacted by Parliament) as well as law interpreted by the courts (case law). Just reading the legislation will sometimes not be sufficient to understand the application of that law. It is the way in which the courts have interpreted the law, especially when decisions have been appealed and heard by courts of higher authority, which provide for a broader understanding of the law.

In the most basic terms, law is the application of a set of rules (laws) to a dispute. This dispute could be between a couple resulting in Family Court action, between two members of the public resulting in civil action, between an individual and the community resulting in proceedings in a criminal court, or some other conflict between two or more parties. The rules applied to these disputes are based on written and case law relevant to that dispute. As a community we want the law to be based on fairness. However, a court can only make a decision on the application of the rules; the concept of fairness has to have been written into the laws by the Parliament. Therefore, an acquittal of someone accused of a serious crime on a "technicality" may be as a result of the way in which the laws were written, and not necessarily on the way in which the court applied those laws. The courts can only apply the rules.

The way in which a court or tribunal operates depends upon the type of court or tribunal, and the jurisdiction within which it operates. The two most widely used are the adversarial and inquiry systems. The adversarial system, commonly seen in criminal and civil courts in Australia, has two or more sides. A neutral party, either a judge or jury, hears the facts and decides on an outcome after the sides of the case have been presented. The best evidence is deemed to win in the case of competing parties, or is deemed to have passed (or failed to pass) the standard of proof in other cases, particularly criminal matters. The judge also has the role of ensuring the case is presented according to legal requirements.

The inquiry method is commonly seen in tribunals and other bodies. The role of the judge (or assessor of fact) is to find out information and make a decision. Some courts may have aspects of both, or the same court may use different systems in different states. For example, the functioning of a children's court may be based on the adversarial model or, depending on the state, it may have powers of inquiry. Similarly, the Family Court was set up to be inquisitorial but it still has a strong adversarial aspect. From a professional's perspective, the experience is likely to feel the same but there are subtle differences, for example, a judge may ask you more questions in the Family Court.

The Rules of the "Game"

Throughout this book, I use the analogy of "a game" to describe the court process. Outlined below are some of the "rules" of the game relevant to expert witnesses.

However, prior to describing these rules, the analogy needs to be qualified. A "game" implies that there are two or more parties willing to play and that one of those parties will "win". In court, one may not be a willing party and in some cases the parties involved will end up with substantial losses, both emotional and financial. I have yet to hear the parties in a marriage break-up come out of a Family Court trial reporting that they were both happy with the decision! On the other hand, like a game, there are clearly defined rules that need to be understood if you want to be successful. Similarly, your performance as a witness is an important element in the outcome.

For readers with a legal background, my intention is not to demean the legal process through the use of this analogy. The purpose is to use a framework that makes sense to a non-legal professional to help explain an alien environment. I would emphasise to all readers that the courts are one of the most serious and formal institutions in our modern society. They need to be treated with respect and dignity.

Apart from formal court rules, there are various "rules" that relate to the court process. In my opinion, those "rules" relevant to the "game" of court, from the perspective of the outsider, are:

1. The court process is fair, efficient and speedy.

2. Legal decisions are based on the appearance of truth.

3. Favourable evidence is that which is the more believable of the two sides.

4. It does not matter what you did, it only matters what you can prove that did.

These four rules are discussed in detail below.

Rule 1 – The court process is fair, efficient and speedy.

Anyone who has been involved in a legal process is probably laughing after reading this rule. A court is not concerned with the concept of fairness, as a layperson would understand the term; a court is concerned with the application of the law to a dispute. As noted earlier, the law consists of a set of rules enacted by Parliament (that is, legislation). Once the rules are formulated, they are used in court. Judges interpret these rules, and people can appeal the judges' decisions. These appeals are heard by higher courts. The process of interpreting, and appealing those interpretations, results in case law. Therefore, over time, the rules written in the legislation are tested by case law. The tested cases become the measure by which all legal decisions are made until new legislation is enacted. It becomes a system of logic, which is concerned with applying rules to make decisions. This may seem like a strange concept but, when you grasp it, it makes dealing with the legal system much easier to understand.

Lawyers will generally see the rules of court as being fair. For example, hearsay rules exist to prevent information, which may be questionable, being used in court. However, from a witness' point of view, if you were told something but were not allowed to rely on it in court, it would seem very unfair. Consequently, community perception of the unfairness of court exists because of the different systems of logic. As a member of the community the more you can understand law as a set of rules applied to a dispute, the easier it is to accept the various anomalies in fairness.

The second part of rule one is that the court is efficient and speedy. Like the concept of fairness, due to misunderstandings and certain practical realities, this is also a fallacy. The court process takes some time to run its course. In my travels around Australia presenting seminars on this topic, I have found surprisingly similar timeframes. In Western Australia and in other jurisdictions, a typical criminal matter of a more serious nature, if the offender pleads not guilty, will take somewhere between 12 and 18 months from the time they were charged to the time they are sentenced after the trial.

A typical civil matter, such as a workers' compensation claim, negligence, or motor vehicle accident claim, will take anywhere from about two to ten years to settle, unless there is a separate system which streamlines the process (such as in worker's compensation). If you work with children in these areas, it may be well over a decade before that case runs to trial. For example, a neurologist specialising in assessing children's head injuries, who does an assessment on a eight year old injured in a car accident, may find themselves in court a decade later (because the lawyers may not even consider settling the case until that child is an adult and the full extent of the damages are known). The report completed by the professional 2009, based on three or four hours of assessment, may not go to trial until 2020!

In the Family Court, if a complex matter involving serious allegations is resolved by trial in less than 12 months, then something unusual will have happened! It generally takes from one to three years from the initial application to when the matter is decided by a trial. For less serious Family Court matters, it currently takes around 12 months from the start of the matter to trial, and can be quicker in expedited trials. An added complication in the Family Court is that particular issues may settle, but the children remain. Matters that were resolved can resurface years later with new issues. Generally these are the more serious cases, but it is not uncommon to have files that were first in court up to ten years ago. From the health practitioner's perspective, any child you have seen in your practice may end up in a Family Court dispute. You could be required to provide information of importance to the trial, even though that child was seen years ago.

For the client, there are advantages and disadvantages to the long timeframes. The main advantage is that people may not be emotionally stable enough to settle early. For example, it takes one or two years to grieve the loss of a major relationship, so early settlement in the Family Court may not reflect the long-term best interests of the parties. Someone feeling guilty about having an affair may make a financial settlement by giving everything to their former partner, only to realise later that this decision was not in their best interests. Similarly, time is required for injuries to stabilise. A neck injury may seem to be stable at 12 months but, if the person knew it was not going to improve any more over the next 5 years, they may not have settled. Some of the disadvantages for the client in relation to long timeframes include: the fact that people may not progress while there are secondary gains from not getting better, the stress of court is extremely high, and the greater the potential to accrue massive legal debt over long periods of time. For the professional having to appear in court, long timeframes seem to hold no special advantages beyond the opportunity to collect more information.

One implication of the slow timeframe is that when you are taking case notes and writing your report, you need to do it in such a way that, in one, three or ten years, your notes must have sufficient information to allow you to give credible evidence, even if you do not specifically remember the case! Politicians can get away with "I don't remember" when asked about past events, but court witnesses are seen as less credible when over-using that excuse.

Rule 2 – Legal decisions are based on the appearance of truth.

To understand this second point, it is important to consider that when the event resulting in court action occurred, the judge, the applicant's lawyer, the respondent's lawyer, nor the jury were present. However, these are the people who will run the process or make the decisions. The judge and jury can only listen to the witnesses who give evidence, and form views about what really happened. They look at the appearance of truth, because they do not have access to the absolute truth.

The way the judge or jury assess the appearance of truth is by assessing the credibility of the witnesses, both ordinary and expert. They also examine documents and tangible evidence to corroborate the different sources of information into a logical whole. This is called the application of forensic logic.

The lawyers try to highlight or discredit the believability – or reliability – of witnesses and other evidence to show which version of the facts is most plausible and consistent. It is not about finding an absolute truth, as in most cases there is no direct discovery of the absolute truth.

Flowing from this aspect of the legal process is the importance of both your personal presentation and the presentation of your evidence as critical factors in the court environment. Later in the book I discuss the things witnesses can do to look presentable and give evidence in a credible fashion.

Rule 3 – Favourable evidence is that which is the more believable of the two sides.

After carefully observing the evidence given by the

witnesses, the judge gains some understanding of what is apparently true. The judge has to decide what he or she believes from the arguments heard and evidence presented. He or she decides the truth based on whom and what was the more believable of the two sides. The process of reaching a conclusion from the available evidence, and then applying the relevant law to those findings, allows the judge to make a decision (or judgment) about a particular matter.

In making the judgment, the judge has to justify the conclusions based on forensic logic, will go through the evidence heard or seen, and will make comments about how important or "material" the evidence appeared. The judge is obliged to give reasons for his or her decision. In doing this the judge may say: "I find Dr Jones a reliable witness" or "I find Dr Jones an unreliable witness". Sometimes they will give a qualified position such as: "I think Dr Jones was a reliable witness but I think he overstated this point or put too much weight on that evidence". Through this process, the judge justifies the decision, including which position was more acceptable.

Rule 4 – It does not matter what you did, it only matters what you can prove you did.

To reach a judgment, the evidence is assessed for credibility, and if credible, accorded significant weight. This is where your records become important. Once you are in the witness box, you need to prove your position. Just knowing you did something is not enough. It becomes a question of your word against someone else's position. The court will find your position more credible if you have handwritten contemporaneous notes or recordings, so you can prove what actually happened to a greater degree of certainty. To be able to use them in court, you have to argue the link between the notes or test results and the relevance to your evidence. The easiest way to do this is to indicate that the notes are to "refresh" your memory. Lawyers may talk about this principle in terms of the "best evidence" rule.

The process you use to record your evidence will be examined closely. For example, when a client is talking, although I write down what are they are saying, I sometimes do not manage to record all of it. I know what the person is telling me but, if I do not have it in my notes, I have a problem. In a particular Family Court case, a Queen's Counsel (QC) asked: "Is this what the person told you?" followed by: "Can you show me where in your notes where he said that?" Had I said: "The person talks faster than I can record", the QC would have said: "So your notes are not reliable, are they Dr Watts?" The message here is; the better your records, the better you will survive the court experience.

Key Points

- In certain respects court is like a game – it has an understandable set of rules and procedures. If you understand the rules, then you can perform better within the system.

- The court is unlike a game in that it is one of our most serious institutions and it makes binding decisions. One does not play games with the court.

- Democracy in Australia works by having the judiciary and the government function as separate systems. Those who make the rules, and those who administer the rules, are separate so they keep each other in check.

- There are two types of rules; those written in the legislation, and the case law which emerges from the testing of the rules.

- The fairness of court is not determined by the court but by the government that wrote the rules. All the court can do is administer the rules.

- The court process is slow. It is important for the professional to understand that material collected for use in court may not be needed for many months or years. Therefore, records or any material collected for court needs to be detailed and very accurate.

- The key decision makers in court do not have access to the absolute truth, as they were not there when the situation occurred. They have to rely on witnesses to determine what happened.

- The believability of the witnesses is critical to the outcome. The court must rely upon the most believable version of events.

- The court will determine the believability of the witnesses. The credibility of the witnesses will be essential to this process.

- Court is an evidence-based system.

- Evidence is based on what you can prove, rather than what you think. Proof of your evidence, (for example, contemporaneous notes, in particular), is of critical value.

- The best evidence is what you can prove by showing it to the court.

2

Pathways to Court

It is essential to understand that the credibility of your evidence depends on how you structure your role from the beginning. The pathway that brought you into court makes a lot of difference. In my opinion, there are three main pathways to court.

The first pathway is that of the forensic expert. Forensic experts are those, like myself, who actively seek work within the legal arena knowing that there is a real possibility that they will give evidence in court. I am amazed at the range of professions that have a forensic branch. Medicine is well-known for its forensic examinations of murder victims. Television shows such as "Profiler" have made the general public aware of forensic psychology or psychiatry. Forensic accounting is also well-known. Accident assessments by engineers may not use the word "forensic" but that is exactly what the assessment is. Even in anthropology there is a forensic group that may review old bones for injuries to indicate cause of death.

A second pathway brings those professionals who do not actively seek court work, but who provide a service of some type, into court. One day you may be peacefully doing your work, only to have a subpoena served upon you. The subpoena demands that you attend court. Alternatively, a lawyer may contact you to say: "I need a report for my client who is your patient or client; will you provide one?" This book has been written primarily for those of you who come into court via this second pathway.

A third way in which you, as a professional, could be drawn into the court system is through a negligence claim. This is the least desirable position to be in. In a negligence situation you are personally on the line because you have either done something wrong or have been accused of doing something wrong.

I have not included the miscellaneous life experiences that may draw people into court. For example, if you were in the process of banking the business takings and witnessed a robbery, you may well be called to give evidence. However, your evidence will be that of a lay witness, not that of a professional or expert witness. In this case, you will only be providing evidence of fact, which is the evidence of what you have seen and heard.

There may be other pathways to court, for example, the pathway resulting from the actions initiated by a professional in an investigative capacity. Workers in a child protection capacity may conduct investigations for the purpose of determining whether a child has been abused. Professionals in these cases initiate legal proceedings rather than provide evidence to existing proceedings. In these cases, although these persons are professional witnesses, they will generally provide evidence of fact generated from their investigations. Opinions will be considered, but are secondary factors.

Court proceedings may also arise as a result of running a business, such as actions relating to debt collection, contract disputes, or employee relations. The skills required in relation to the presentation of evidence are similar, but the evidence will be largely about fact, not professional opinion.

In the following sections, various aspects of opinion evidence will be discussed in detail. Although you may be a treatment provider rather than a forensic expert, it is important to structure your approach to the evidence as if you were a forensic expert. In my opinion, it is of crucial importance that you understand the principles that underlie the way in which forensic experts conduct their practice if you are going to survive the court system.

Forensic Experts

Within the court system, a forensic expert can be appointed in a number of ways. The following hierarchy shows the most to the least desirable position in terms of your independence (and therefore the perceived strength of your evidence):

Court-appointed expert

Agreed expert

Party expert

Paper (theoretical) expert

Critique opinion expert

Court-appointed Experts

Under various laws, courts have the ability to appoint

their own expert. The Family Court uses many experts; for example, the court will regularly appoint mental health professionals to talk to children and/or assess parents with respect to the children, and will appoint accountants and evaluators to assist with financial matters. Other courts may have the capacity to appoint an expert, but it is an option that is rarely used except in the case of children's courts. I am aware of a recent exception; a negligence case involving a neuropsychological assessment. Two of my colleagues had assessed a client and subsequently gave evidence in court. One colleague gave evidence for the plaintiff and the other for the insurance company. The judge said: "I need another opinion", so he appointed a third colleague to provide another opinion. The judge accepted the third opinion. He had appointed an independent psychologist in addition to the professionals who had already been retained by the parties to the action. In a civil court, such an approach is rare.

As a court-appointed expert, you are in a position of strength because you are in fact considered to be an officer of the court. You are working for the court so your role is seen as neutral and independent. To be seen as independent is an advantage when commencing to provide your evidence. At the conclusion of your evidence, you may still be perceived as biased, but that would be due to your approach and presentation, not your role. Your ability to be seen as independent, and not influenced by a particular bias, determines how credible the court perceives you to be. In other words, the protection afforded to a court expert is limited by the extent to which your biases influence your evidence. This will be explored further in chapter four.

One of the ironies of this is that the greater your involvement with the court the less likely it will be that you will have to give evidence. In Western Australia I have been appointed as a court-appointed expert in over 600 Family Court matters. Less than two out of every ten of these messy, complex family assessments end up in trial. Why? Because I am independent (that is, not appointed by either of the parties), the judges place a certain level of significance upon my views. In circumstances in which I am asked to assess a parent only, about 50 per cent of those cases end up in trial. Why? My evidence is not given as much weight in these cases because I may be perceived to "work for" one party only; as such, the parties do not reach agreement.

Agreed Experts

The next highest level of independence is that of the agreed expert. The two opposing parties may request an independent assessment (in the absence of a court order to legitimise the role). As an agreed expert you are considered to be independent, but you are not an officer of the court. Therefore, with respect to independence, it is a similar position to that of a court-appointed expert but the evidence is not as powerful.

In my experience this type of appointment occurs when the lawyers for each of the parties know each other and know my work. As an independent expert, your evidence is much stronger than that of the next category of expert, the party expert.

Party Experts

A party expert is someone who agrees to work for one party (side) to provide a report. Someone wants an opinion and they have asked you for it. The problem with this is that you are likely to be seen by the court as either biased or lacking counter-information to reach a balanced view. You may be the most independent professional in the world, but because you work for one side only, the court may perceive you to have a bias.

To maximise your usefulness, it is important to manage the process of your appointment. There are many subtle ways of doing this, for example, by requesting to be subpoenaed. Subpoenas are discussed later in more detail, however, the following example illustrates their effect. I was once asked to provide a forensic assessment as a court-appointed expert. The father involved in the case had been convicted for some extremely violent assaults. He had taken his former de facto by gunpoint into the hills and, before she managed to escape, sexually and physically assaulted her and threatened to kill her. He was eventually gaoled but, after his release, he went to her house and did the same thing again, but on this occasion he had a knife. Obviously, this was someone with a significant pathology of risk. When I carried out the assessment for the Family Court I concluded that for various reasons there should not be any contact between this man and his child. It was a standard assessment by a court-appointed expert.

Several years later the woman asked me to give evidence at a restraining order hearing. Her former partner was to be paroled and the law at that time offered no automatic protection to her. The law required that she apply for a court order (the laws were subsequently amended and now victims of serious crime receive automatic protection). I said that I was willing to appear in court but I requested that she subpoena me. Why the subpoena? If I had attended court as her witness, I may have been seen to be biased (as I had been involved in a previous matter relating to the same parties). In addition, because I had collected the evidence while a court-appointed expert, I may also have had problems with respect to confidentiality. A subpoena would enable me to attend court and retain a role as a court-appointed expert. For example, I could say: "I didn't do this assessment for her, Your Honour, I did it for the Family Court as a court expert and this is what I found ...". The subpoena provided me with a level of independence greater than that of a party expert and to a level almost as high as that of a court-appointed expert. Irrespective of your profession, if you collect evidence in one forum, and it is to be used in another, look for ways to increase your integrity within the process.

If you are going to work as a party expert, it is important to acknowledge your limitations. The court needs to know the basis of your evidence. Highlight any significant limitations in your evidence. It is important to say: "I have seen X but I have not seen Y". It is also important to state which documents you have read or the people you have interviewed. If you go to court and a lawyer says: "You did not see Y, did you?" and you say "no" and they ask: "Well, should you?", you can respond by saying: "I have outlined in my report why I did not". The court is then in a position to determine whether or not you have done your job carefully and whether you have considered other options knowing that you lacked certain pieces of information.

Paper (Theoretical) Experts

For want of a better name, a paper expert is someone who offers a theoretical view on a topic but generally does not see anyone. It is a theoretical opinion only – a dry academic review. It does not matter what area you specialise in – it might be as obscure as people's phobic reactions to pigeons – sooner or later some lawyer will require an expert opinion on phobic reactions to pigeons.

They will ask your colleagues until they find someone, whether a practitioner or an academic researcher, who can answer the questions they need answered. Some examples of situations in which I have acted as a "paper expert" and offered to provide an opinion to the Family Court include: the capability of homosexual men to be parents, Battered Wife Syndrome, the existence of Post-Traumatic Stress Disorder (although with the DSM-IV that is a reasonably easy argument to make), and the ages (in theory) at which children best cope with overnight contact with a parent. Other examples include: an engineer providing differing models for the calculation of concrete pours; a mining engineer providing an opinion in relation to depreciation models for mine construction equipment; and an electrical engineer explaining the difference between copper cable and optic fibre in a dispute with the Australian Taxation Office in relation to GST.

When offering an opinion on a topic in isolation, there are several major issues to consider. The first is to ensure that you really are an expert in the subject before you offer the opinion. Second, ensure that you clearly spell out your limitations in the report. Third, and in many ways this is the most important consideration, stay within the bounds of what you know and do not speculate on other areas. If you are careful to stay within the bounds of your expertise, the information provided may be of vital importance to the court. On the other hand, paper opinions may be perceived to have no substance, because you have not evaluated all of the variables in the case.

In an interesting example a lawyer asked if I could provide a critique of an American article. The article offered some theoretical criteria used to determine whether someone had sex offender characteristics. After I reviewed the article the lawyer asked if I would assess his client against the criteria. Unfortunately, the client matched every one of the theoretic risk factors! I had to contact the lawyer and explain that if I provided a report it would not be of any use to the defence case. I subsequently provided a pre-sentence report after the man was convicted of the offences.

Critique Opinion Experts

A critique opinion expert is someone who provides an opinion on another professional's report. A critique opinion expert should not be confused with a genuine second opinion. A second opinion is actually an opinion provided by a party expert because they have seen the client, or evaluated the issues in real life, for one party to the dispute. A professional has written a report based on an assessment – you then examine it to offer a critique of the strengths and weaknesses of both the assessment and the report. In that role the court may see you as both biased and limited because you have not assessed anybody yourself. All you have done is comment on the way in which your colleague carried out their task.

There is a place for this type of review but you should be very aware of the potential problems. It is not a time to get personal or to promote a particular agenda. It is essential that you focus on aspects such as the methodology, the approach, the logic in the other professional's reasoning, and whether their findings are reasonable. Do not make statements such as: "This person is an idiot and does not know what they are talking about". Do not engage in personal attacks, nor criticise their areas of expertise. Base your critique on the content and process, not the person. This approach is important, not only for reasons of professional courtesy but also because an attack on another professional tends to weaken your own credibility.

If your report is critiqued, consider carefully whether you should even respond. Your natural inclination may be to write a detailed rebuttal. All that does is provide the lawyers with ammunition to use against you. On one occasion, upon returning from a five-week absence, I received three critiques of different comprehensive assessments I had conducted as a court-appointed expert. I took the first critique very seriously and, in my stressed state, I wrote approximately 25 pages in response to the criticism. I was advised by a lawyer not to respond to the other two critiques. Instead, I wrote a simple response saying: "I do not think the criticisms are valid and I am willing to address them at trial". As a strategy it worked well in that particular case. Note that I received legal advice before acting in that instance. In a different situation, another strategy may have been warranted.

Alternatively, rather than offering a critique opinion, I sometimes provide lawyers with a cross-examination strategy. Lawyers may find this useful, as they often do not understand concepts or terminology relating to other professions. This approach helps them to understand what the professional is saying. I have at times been amazed at a lawyer's lack of understanding of another profession's terminology. In one case in which the lawyers read a neurological report, they did not realise that it said that the person had brain damage from an acquired injury! I am not trained in neurology, however, I was still able to be of assistance. In the role of critique opinion expert, I interpret what the professional is saying and highlight the strengths and weaknesses of the report. Lawyers can find that very useful but your colleagues may not.

If you are going to prepare a critique opinion report, make sure that you determine whether you are actually allowed to see the report. Some courts have specific rules in relation to the release of their reports without an order of the court. On one occasion in which I wrote a report for the Family Court, my report was sent to a colleague by one of the parties requesting that the colleague see the children and then critiques my report. My colleague was not familiar with the intricacies of the Family Court. When he subsequently provided evidence at trial, the judge berated him sternly because he had both read the report and had seen the children without the Court's permission (a court order prevented the children from being seen by another professional without the approval of the court). Ignorance of matters such as these is no defence. With respect to the Family Court of Australia, an expert preparing material should be familiar with Part 15 of the Family Law Rules 2004 (Cwlth), which refers to expert evidence. Other courts also have rules relating to the provision of expert evidence. Each court usually provides access to their rules and procedures on their respective Internet websites.

If in doubt about the rules for releasing reports, there are some simple strategies to adequately address consent issues. If a client wants to give you a report directly, you should refuse to accept it and instead request that their lawyer send it to you. The court will assume that the lawyer would have obtained the necessary permissions before sending a copy to you. When I write these reports, I often state: "This report was provided by such and such solicitor. I assume they have the necessary releases for me to have seen the report". Who will the judge blame if there are problems? The lawyer is more likely to be in the firing line to receive any criticism, not you as the recipient of the report.

I avoid having clients give me documents for several reasons. Sometimes clients will provide documents which are considered to be very prejudiced or that you should not see. In one case, in the middle of my evidence, I made a passing comment that I had seen a particular document. The judge immediately stopped the trial. I was then sent out of the court while they debated whether or not I should have seen the document. At the end of the debate they decided I should not have seen it and subsequently disqualified all of my evidence. The moral here is to be very careful about the information you use and how you get it. Most of the time it will not be a problem, but be cautious in your approach, because there are intricacies in the rules of evidence that can affect you. On the other hand, not seeing particular material may jeopardise the usefulness of your evidence. It is important therefore not to ignore useful information because of concerns about admissibility.

Forensic Experts and Personal Risk

If you are going to work as a forensic expert, you should remember that you will often work with clients who may be disturbed, highly stressed and/or very angry. In simple terms, reasonable people usually solve their problems without having to go to court. In the legal arena some of the people have pathologies that make them unreasonable. This includes short-term stress relating to the situation, personality disorders, certain intellectual or cognitive limitations, or mental illnesses. Some people may have been convicted previously of violent acts or they may suffer significant stress from being in the legal system. A few of those people may still be very dangerous. Personally, I have not received death threats, however, I did have a stalker for many years, one of my colleagues had a man visit his office and threaten to kill him, and another colleague was murdered. While considering your risk, it is important not to lose sight of the fact that there are many socially appropriate and reasonable people who need help, so do not assume that everyone is bad.

It is important to consider the possibility that some of your clients may have psychological and other disturbances, and to structure your practice accordingly. I have a home office, which I use on a limited basis, with my main consulting rooms located elsewhere. I do not carry out any criminal or Family Court assessments from my home office because it is too risky. The only clients I see in my home office are those who have been screened carefully.

Key Points

- The structure of the role at the beginning of the process is critical for the quality of the evidence at the end.

- There are three main pathways for a professional to provide opinion evidence in court: as a forensic expert who anticipates working within the legal system; as a service provider who inadvertently ends up in court; or through negligence claims raised in relation to their work.

- Other aspects of business practice may lead to court. This includes debt collection, contract disputes, and industrial relations, but these appearances will be for the purpose of providing evidence of fact rather than opinion.

- It is preferable to give evidence as a court-appointed expert. This is because you are not considered to be taking anyone's side and you are effectively acting as an officer of the court.

- Working for a party (one side) may be unavoidable but you should consider if there are ways to be more independent.

- Other forensic roles, such as providing critiques of reports, theoretical evidence or models, are necessary services for the legal profession. Be very careful not to overstep the evidence, or to address substantive issues beyond the evidence base. Take care not to let personal issues interfere with the role you are undertaking.

Service Provider Issues

The Role of the Service Provider

Any professional who may be required to give evidence needs to understand the principles applicable to the forensic expert, because those principles are directly relevant to being a credible witness. However, for the professional whose practice is concerned with providing treatment or services, and not specifically concerned with providing assessments for court, there are other issues to consider. As a service provider you are doing what you have been trained to do, that is, to provide some type of service that was not necessarily intended to have a legal purpose. However, out of the blue, you may find yourself involved in the legal system; for example, a client may request a report, a client's lawyer might contact you to request a report, or a subpoena may be delivered to your office.

Sometimes lawyers use cunning means to obtain the information they need. For example, most lawyers know that service providers hate going to court. If a lawyer contacts a service provider to say: "I have a client I want you to see for a particular service or treatment so you can give us a report for court", they might receive the response: "No thanks, we do not do legal work, send them to somebody else". As a result, lawyers use alternative strategies, such as one I experienced recently. I received a letter in which the first sentence read: "We arranged for Donna X to attend at your Mount Pleasant office on 19th December. As you may not be aware,

we act for Donna and her mother in a claim against ...".
What the lawyers had done was to send this lady to see
me as a treating psychologist but with the deliberate
intention of obtaining a report. There have been
attempts by professional societies in some states to set
up agreements with the relevant law societies to try to
stop this sort of conduct. I believe that the original model
resulted from an agreement between the Australian
Medical Association (AMA) and the New South Wales
Law Society. I have observed that such agreements or
codes of practice appear to make a difference; however, I
would be surprised if the backdoor approaches stopped
completely.

A service provider may end up in court in a variety of
ways. The following sections describe the main pathways
into court. Unlike the pathways to court for forensic
experts, those in the following list have no particular
advantage over one another:

Party requested

Family Court

Subpoenas

Other pathways

Before discussing the details of these pathways, it is
worth noting the basic difference in position between that
of a service provider and a forensic expert. The difference
centres upon the awareness of the issues in question.
The forensic expert knows what questions are being
asked, and therefore they have the luxury of conducting
a comprehensive assessment that attempts to cover all
of the main possibilities. The service provider collects
information relevant to the service or treatment provided,
and therefore may not have the knowledge to answer the
lawyer's question without seeing the client again.

Party Requested

The role of the party expert has been described previously. The difference here is that it is an existing or former client who will request information for the court. A party expert is one who begins a new assessment with the particular issues of the dispute in mind. As a person appearing at the request of one of the parties in a legal dispute, you may be seen to be biased. You may be a good practitioner, but there are pros and cons to entering the legal arena at the request of a party. Some workers in the forensic area argue about whether service providers should ever be called to give evidence. This is a loaded debate beyond the scope of this book but you should be aware of the pitfalls if you are to avoid them.

The obvious advantage of the service professional giving evidence is that they see a client for a much longer period of time and get to know them better. The disadvantage is that they take on a sort of ownership of the client or work task, which may affect their ability to be seen to be independent. Another disadvantage is you may not have examined specifically the question the lawyer is asking of you. When in court, expect questions suggesting that you are biased, working for a particular person, or addressing other issues in relation to your objectivity.

I have a mixed practice and I therefore see clients for both treatment and forensic assessments. I would argue that I have different approaches to my forensic assessment and clinical work. I make a conscious effort to think differently. The mindset I have with a clinical client is that I believe what they tell me, but I look for any inconsistencies and I give them feedback about these. If I am conducting a forensic assessment, I work from the position that I am sceptical about what they are telling me and I look for consistencies within the story and data. I do not give the client feedback during the assessment, which is important as feedback may lead the client to respond in beneficial ways. In effect I am building a bottom-up picture for a forensic assessment, whereas in clinical practice it is a top-down process. Obviously the same scenario might apply to other professions. For example, an accountant may be protective of their business client in a way that is very different to the way in which they would approach a forensic evaluation of a business.

A different issue for the service providing professional is the impact of the legal process on the therapeutic relationship. If you are treating someone, and write a report about them, it could jeopardise your relationship with that client in future sessions. I have had clients who have refused to come back and see me after I have put my opinions in writing. For example, a physiotherapist might say to a patient: "Your back problem is made worse because have a long-standing pattern of difficulty dealing with stress". The patient happily agrees with the statement. In a legal report the physiotherapist writes: "The client's emotional issues are interfering with the recovery due to psychosomatic processes". The client may never want to return to the physiotherapist (for example, after looking up the meaning of the report on the Internet). On the other hand, some clients do come back and say that you provided a great report and that they are happy but, more often than not, the client will cease treatment (or if they continue to receive treatment, the relationship will be strained). It is a double bind in that the more you write a report in order to help the client or patient, the more the court will see you as biased.

There are ways to deal with the process to maximise the chances of keeping the client-practitioner relationship functioning in a therapeutic way. First, find out whether the requested report is actually needed. Contact the lawyer to discuss the issues. The lawyer is interested in obtaining evidence but may be sensitive to your issues if you explain that you may not be able to help the client after the report is released. You can suggest that the lawyer obtain a forensic assessment from someone else who may be more independent (you, as the client's service provider, may be seen to be taking a biased position). If a lawyer believes you are biased, they will probably drop you like a hot potato. Too many service providers, upon receipt of a letter from a lawyer requesting a report, simply provide the report without questioning the value of it with the lawyer.

Another useful approach is to discuss the report with the client before you write it, and to go over the draft report before it is released. Addressing the issues in person often helps to resolve the problem, prevent the client from misunderstanding the jargon, and also provide you with an opportunity to explain your rationale. In this day and age of privacy legislation, it is critical that the client is aware of your report and that you have obtained the necessary written permission to release it.

Assuming you cannot negotiate yourself out of the need for providing a report, the best guidance I can offer is to understand the difference between being a "witness of fact" and an "expert witness". This point is discussed in various places in this book but in summary, a witness of fact can report what they have seen, heard or done. An expert witness can offer an opinion about the dynamics or reasons for the particular behaviour. As a treating professional, describing a symptom tends to provide evidence of a fact. The more you offer diagnosis and supposition for behaviour, the more you offer opinion rather than fact. If in doubt, stick to the facts and avoid opinions.

Furthermore, there is a helpful distinction to be made with opinion: there are diagnostic and substantive opinions. The more a service provider limits themselves to the diagnostic opinion and fact, the better. Leave the substantive opinion about wider case issues to the independent experts.

A final point of caution is in relation to the blurring of the role between forensic evaluation and service provision in your practice. If providing a service, stick with service issues and recognise your limitations. If conducting a forensic evaluation, do not also take on a service provider role for a party, as this will significantly weaken your independence.

Family Court

The Family Court has to make decisions about complex family breakdowns involving all sorts of problems – parents who cannot resolve their problems, concerns about the welfare of children, issues surrounding domestic violence, drug treatment, intellectual difficulties, head injuries in accidents, psychiatric or medical illnesses, personality disorders, allegations of sexual abuse, or people who have come to the notice of major government departments for various reasons. The court also needs financial information, evaluations, tax, superannuation and other types of advice. Evidence from the agencies and professionals involved may help to shed light on the central issues of the case. For example, the couple's interaction style noted by a treating therapist three years prior to a marital break-up may be critical in determining whether current allegations of domestic violence have been exaggerated for the court or are a well-documented problem of many years' duration.

Under the Family Law Rules 2004 (Cwlth), there is a clearly expressed difference in the court's expectations in relation to a treating professional and an expert providing a report for the parties. If the treatment precedes the request for information, and the information required is limited to evidence of facts or opinions solely about treatment, then Part 15.5 (in relation to expert evidence) may not apply. If you are drawn into comments about parenting issues, then the Rules may apply. If the lawyer talks to you about providing a report in relation to non-treatment issues, providing an assessment of the parties, or if you have not yet seen the parties, then the Rules could well apply. Among the requirements in the Rules are for all communications between the lawyer and professional to be in writing, and that the permission of the court may be needed before the information can be used. Therefore, you should request written information from the lawyer immediately and respond to the lawyer in writing. The situation is less obvious if the person is self-represented. Ensure that you request information in writing, as the self-represented person may not be aware of the Rules.

In Western Australia, as in most states, there is a practice of issuing subpoenas to any professional who may have some information about the parties on their files. Whatever your area of work, you are likely to find that you will eventually receive a subpoena to produce evidence to a court. This includes evidence from bankers, accountants, financial planners, doctors, schoolteachers, speech therapists, psychologists, medical doctors, hospital workers.

Subpoenas

A subpoena is a legal demand to provide information. It has a status similar to that of other court orders. The court takes compliance with subpoenas very seriously. If the court cannot force people to meet its needs, then the constitutional independence of the legal system is threatened. Therefore, if you do not attend court, or fail to get the subpoena put aside, a warrant for your arrest may be issued – you may be held in prison and brought to court on a day –by day basis to give your evidence. This is of course an extreme example of what happens if you do not comply, but the legal system has significant coercive power under the law to ensure compliance with a subpoena.

In the Family Court, subpoenas are routine documents but still have to be taken seriously. If you are a "friendly" witness, after a request from a lawyer, the subpoena might just arrive in the mail. In other cases the subpoena has to be "served" on you. When it is served, it has to be done in person and in a particular way.

The first thing to do when you get a subpoena is to read it carefully. Why do I say carefully? The subpoena may request an attendance in person or it might just be a request to produce documents. I have heard of colleagues attending court when all they needed to do was to send documents. If the subpoena says on it "documents", the file and any other requested documents should be sent. If it says "person", then you are required to attend court (the issue of privileged information will be addressed later). If it states both, then you send the file and attend court.

The language of lawyers is very precise. They are likely to request that you include all records, including electronic communications. What is an electronic communication? Obviously faxes are an electronic communication. Email is also an electronic communication. Do you include a hard copy of emails on your file? I did not, thinking that I could just print them off as needed (supporting the paperless society), but then my computer crashed which resulted in a loss of three years worth of email communication. Not nice! Have you considered that SMS and other text messages via a telephone are also electronic communications? It is possible, using software, to download these from most modern phones. As technology changes, there will be various other forms of electronic communications, which will also need to be put on file.

Another aspect of reading the documents with carefully is to ensure that you only comply with what has been requested. A subpoena may be for limited materials and provision of additional materials may not only be unnecessary but may be a legal breach of privacy. By way of example, I had a subpoena which requested release of all documents related to "treatment" of a particular client. However, I had only ever assessed him and I had not provided treatment. The strict interpretation of the subpoena required that I did not release that information.

While subpoena law varies in Australia from state to state and from court to court, it is generally permissible to provide a copy of your documents rather than the originals. I recently received a subpoena from New South Wales in relation to a workers' compensation matter. The subpoena specifically requested a copy of my documents and money had been provided to cover the cost of the photocopying. In Western Australia, the last subpoena I received did not specify "copy", however, upon investigation I was advised that copies were permissible. In some states or courts you might have to provide certified copies of your documents. You will need to use a Justice of the Peace (or another type of authorised person, depending on what the court requires) and have that person certify that the copies are true and correct copies of the original documents. In other cases, it is enough to have a copy of a document accompanied by a letter saying: "I certify that this is an original copy". As noted elsewhere in this book, it may be necessary to obtain legal advice to find out the appropriate procedures in your state (or in relation to a particular court). If you are unsure of what is required, find out from somebody who knows.

There are several reasons why I prefer to provide copies of documents when subpoenaed. First of all, the Registry of the Court receiving the file will often hold it for a very long time. They may have the file for as long as 12 months or more. Imagine the situation where you have to go to court to give evidence and you do not have your file. A second reason why I copy the file, especially in relation to the Family Court, is that if you have the original file you can see if someone has altered your notes (on the copy). This is not common but I do know of a case where one of the parties went through a doctor's subpoenaed file and actually changed some of the details. In addition, I often number the file's pages sequentially because sometimes entire pages go missing.

An interesting aspect of subpoena law is in relation to conduct money. This is something that may be specific to particular courts but, by law, when a subpoena is served they have to provide you with enough money to attend court (called conduct money). This rule is designed for general witnesses to prevent them using the excuse that they could not afford to get to court. For example, under Schedule 4 of the Family Law Rules 2004 (Cwlth) a witness must be paid a minimum of $10, but the rules also include provisions for accommodation, meals and return costs if the witness has to travel over certain distances. However, if the conduct money is not provided when it is supposed to have been provided, then the subpoena may be deemed to have been served incorrectly. In one particular case I used this avenue to get out of attending court. However, I only did this after obtaining legal advice as this is a complex area of the law (penalties apply if you get it wrong).

One of my colleagues thought that conduct money was all she could get paid. My understanding is that you can be paid a reasonable professional fee, over and above conduct money, for complying with a subpoena. For example, in the

Family Court of Western Australia's information it states: "You may be entitled to recover reasonable costs incurred [in] complying with a subpoena; You should advise the requesting party the estimated reasonable cost in writing as soon as possible. If there is a dispute, the court can be asked to make a ruling". I was sent a cheque for $25 with a New South Wales subpoena to produce documents for the District Court. They had a prescribed schedule of fees. In general, in most Western Australian courts, there is no preset schedule for mental health professionals who comply with subpoenas. Areas such as workers' compensation are generally those that are most likely to have prescribed fee schedules. If there is a dispute about payment, the court can make a ruling on what is a reasonable fee.

Generally the party who has subpoenaed you is the party who is responsible for the costs, whether or not they originally engaged your services. The legal profession has clearly defined rules and protocols for these types of issues but, unless you know what they are, you have to ensure that you cover yourself. As a result, the first thing I do when I get a subpoena for attending court is to write to the requesting party outlining what my reasonable costs are. Sometimes, when the party is self-represented and they find out that they are responsible for costs, they cancel the attendance. Once it is in writing, it is easier to argue that the fees were reasonable and agreed, because they were known prior to providing the evidence.

It is important to check the times and dates listed on the subpoena. A request for attendance in person is almost always worded in the legal equivalent to "9am [or whatever time the court starts] on the first morning and day by day thereafter to the conclusion of trial". In reality, the court will almost never want you at 9am on the first day because the lawyers first have to give their opening arguments (unless you are contesting the subpoena, in which case they will want to hear these arguments before the trial commences in earnest). If you contact the lawyer who subpoenaed you to ask when they will want you, they will usually be helpful and give you an estimated time. They become even more helpful if you indicate that you charge the standard fee for the time you make yourself available to the court. They will not want you sitting around for days at a cost of several hundred dollars per hour.

If you are a layperson called as a witness, the court may expect you to sit there from 9am on the first day. The whole reason for this approach is that court process is very expensive – the judge, the judge's associate, and a multitude of lawyers and barristers are all very costly to keep waiting around for witnesses. Everything revolves around the court's convenience. They line up the witnesses outside the courtroom, so as soon as one is finished the next one can slot in, much like a production line. Therefore, they may request you to attend at particular time, but can only estimate when your slot in the production line will come up. As a professional person, if you talk to the briefing lawyer or trial barrister, in many cases they will interpose you. This means that they put you in at an agreed time, which is mutually convenient. In a four- or five-day trial, they work out roughly when they want you and you then attend at the fixed time. It does not always happen on time, and you may still end up waiting, but it is very rare that I have had to spend more than half a day waiting at court.

Sometimes I am asked whether we need to get the details of a court attendance in writing. My experience is that a verbal agreement is generally good enough but, if you think you are dealing with a law firm that may not follow-up with your payment, it is good practice to get the details confirmed in writing. I do not have to be paranoid about these issues, as most of the law firms I have dealt with are reasonable and fair in dealing with a professional witness.

I try to avoid making legal arrangements directly through the client unless they are self-represented. I never accept information from a client who says: "I spoke to my lawyer and you are needed on Wednesday". It is best to contact the lawyer.

Sometimes I think professionals are scared of talking to lawyers. If you contact a lawyer, they are usually only too happy to talk to you. If they have subpoenaed you, you can say: "yes, I have got this information" or "no, I haven't". I advised a friend recently whom the side in opposition to her client subpoenaed. My advice was to ring the subpoenaing lawyer and ask what information was required. She rang them and, when she told them she did not have the required information, they told her to forget the subpoena. She, of course, then asked for written confirmation that the subpoena had been cancelled.

There are certain limits to subpoenas. If the subpoena is "onerous" you do not have to comply. How to define "onerous" can be quite tricky and this is a sign that legal advice is required. I once received a subpoena requesting my case notes and "every article on parental alienation sent to me by the Legal Aid Commission of Western Australia". I wrote a letter in reply stating that I knew that Legal Aid had sent me some articles on parental alienation, but that I did not know how many articles they had sent to me, and finally noted that the articles were now in my general library of articles on Family Court issues. After receiving some legal advice, I sent in my clinical file and the letter. I never heard another word about it.

The timeframe is another limit to a subpoena. If the subpoena is issued with an unreasonable timeframe within which to comply, you may have grounds for non-compliance. I would recommend seeking legal advice before responding: "You gave me only 24 hours so I did not comply". The other implication resulting from non-compliance due to short timeframes is that the judge may not see you as being overly helpful to the court. Therefore, technically it may be sufficient not to comply but how will the judge assess you if you; a) bent over backwards to comply, or b) held up court for months because they did not have your information?

A trap worth noting is that of compliance on THREAT of subpoena. A lawyer may contact you along the following lines: "We are going to subpoena your notes, so can you send them to us now?" I knew of a colleague who did that, but she never actually received the subpoena. A very disgruntled, but justified, client may have had grounds to make a claim against the professional through both the Registration Board and Office of the Federal Privacy Commissioner (who handles complaints pursuant to the Privacy Act 1988 (Cwlth)). A correctly served subpoena, not the threat of a subpoena, is required before you act.

It is important that you keep on file the original subpoena with the court stamp on it. At the risk of generating paranoia unnecessarily, I once had a case in which a mother, in a Family Court matter, had cut, pasted and photocopied orders (to make them read like real orders) but left out the bits that did not suit her! The bottom line is that you need to check your local rules and procedures in relation to subpoenas (including correct service), as it will be you who will be held accountable if a dispute emerges.

In relation to confidentiality, all service providers, including health professionals, have a hard time arguing that information obtained from a client is confidential. Generally speaking, the information is not confidential. If you try to claim privilege over that information, it is important to know that this is a complex area of law and therefore it is essential that you seek legal advice. There are, however, areas in which I have successfully argued that information is privileged (and therefore successfully objected to the subpoena). One area related to the protection of psychological test material on a file. I argued that the validity of psychological tests could be damaged if they were made publicly available, so I requested that my psychological testing results only be released to another psychologist. This approach has been upheld not only in Australia but also in other parts of the world. This concept may have relevance to other professions if the tests would lose their validity if made widely available.

Materials, such as psychological tests, may also have other restrictions, such as copyright, covering their use. If you copy or release test results and, in particular, if you reveal test items, obtain legal advice about psychological testing first. This is because a valid subpoena may not protect you from your professional obligations. For example, you may be expected to request the court to withhold the disclosure of test items from the court's judgment. There is every reason to expect that the same principles will apply to tests purchased and used by other professions.

A second area in which I have successfully objected to a subpoena related to the provision of marriage counselling to a couple who subsequently separated. The first party (the husband) requested information from my file for the purposes of a matter before a criminal court. The second party (the wife) was no longer involved in the first party's life. I argued successfully that reference to the second party in information on that file would, if released, be an unnecessary breach of confidentiality. Confidentiality may also be protected in relation to certain registered counsellors who provide counselling protected under specific legislative provisions (discussed below).

The way in which privilege is structured will vary from court to court. In the marriage counselling example just described, I provided a complete set of my file notes in a sealed envelope marked "Privilege". A copy of the notes, with the privileged sections blanked out, was placed in the court's main file. On the first day of the trial a lawyer raised the issue of privilege on my behalf. Had he failed, the court would have opened the envelope and made the full notes available.

The information of some government departments and agencies is accorded privilege pursuant to various Acts of Parliament. For example, in Australia certain types of counselling services provided by nominated agencies are unreportable. If you work in these agencies your notes cannot be subpoenaed, but you may be required to provide dates of consultations. However, information obtained by many other government departments, such as welfare, education and health, can be subpoenaed. If you work within the public sector, and you receive a subpoena, you will need to seek advice from your department or agency before complying with the subpoena.

Other Pathways

There are other pathways leading to an appearance in court or similar body. These include commonwealth bodies such as the Administrative Appeals Tribunal, the Migration Review Tribunal, the Refugee Review Tribunal, the Australian Industrial Relations Commission, and Social Security Appeals Tribunal. State courts and tribunals include environmental courts, coroner's courts, industrial commissions and administrative appeals tribunals. These bodies will require information to assist in their decision-making process. The strength of their request for information, and the standard of proof required, will vary depending upon the legislation governing the particular body.

Key Points

- The service provider should consider whether they should provide a report when requested, and they may wish to discuss their issues and concerns with the lawyer making the request.

- In writing a report, a service provider should focus on facts and diagnostic opinion, and minimise comment about substantive opinions in relation to the case.

- The Family Court increasingly seeks information from a variety of professionals, including bankers, accountants, health care providers, childcare workers, and teachers. Consider the request for information carefully and seek legal advice prior to releasing any information.

- Subpoenas must be dealt with, however, this is a complex area of law and therefore you should seek legal and professional advice before complying with any requests for sensitive information.

- Do not release information on a threat of subpoena.

- Avoid taking instructions or making arrangements with any of the parties directly. It is preferable to be instructed by their solicitor. If a party is self-represented, it falls upon you to manage the legal processes, so take extra care in these cases.

- Keep good records of all consultations and interventions. Ensure that copies of electronic records, such as emails and SMS, are put on file.

- Advise the parties in writing of any costs associated with the production of records or attendance at court and, as soon as practicable, ensure you or your organisation receives the appropriate financial reimbursement.

- Be aware of any information on your files that may be privileged, protected, or covered by copyright.

Negligence

The worst possible scenario for any professional is to encounter the court system due to an accusation of wrongdoing. This will place your income, assets, career and reputation on the line. Unfortunately, I have had more formal training in relation to negligence in the process of becoming a diving instructor, than I have had through my training in psychology. In the diving industry you are trained in what constitutes negligence and how to avoid it. The situation in other professions varies widely. My contact with the medical profession has shown that there is a comprehensive focus on risk management, while in other areas of allied health there appears to be varying, but often inadequate, amounts of training on these issues. Other professionals, such as engineers and accountants, are dependent upon their university training, which generally includes some training in negligence.

I read recently that Sydney is now second only to California in litigation (that is, numbers of matters litigated). Whether or not that is fact or fiction there is no doubt that Australians will not hesitate to litigate to resolve disputes, and that this behaviour is increasing steadily. Consequently, as practitioners, we need to understand what constitutes negligence and therefore the types of actions that may lead to court action. To understand negligence it is necessary to understand the concept of the "reasonably prudent person" (RPP) (as referred to in American law) or the "reasonable man or woman" (as referred to in

Australian law). As a teaching tool, the former provides a clearer concept although the meaning of the two phrases is essentially the same. In the case of a psychologist, a reasonable prudent person is a fictitious ideal psychologist who always uses due care and always acts prudently in any and every circumstance. This composite of best practice is what a psychologist will be judged against. The same principle applies to counsellors, social workers, doctors, engineers and other professionals.

One definition of negligence is: "an unintentional fault, or carelessness resulting in injury. It deals with avoidable incidents which should have been anticipated and prevented by taking reasonable precautions" (Cohen, 1995).

In many aspects of the literature of service provision, there are "best practice" models. These are all very interesting in theory, but most of us use personalised variations of the main techniques. Many mainstream treatments, such as hypnosis, acupuncture and chiropractic treatment, were controversial for decades before finally being accepted. Had I used hypnosis 20 years ago, I would have been in a minority within the psychology profession. It is only because of a handful of dedicated practitioners that hypnosis survived as a psychological treatment. Creativity in the face of the majority in a profession may expose someone to litigation, but it is a necessary part of the development of any profession to have pioneers of new techniques who shun the conventional techniques of the day.

Within many professions there is a lack of agreement in relation to the techniques that work. How then will the RPP be judged? The answer is that most professions agree on the way in which their practitioners should conduct themselves. This standardised conduct is referred to by variety of names, but includes ethics, standards, and codes of conduct. Whether or not someone is a member of their professional organisation, they are likely to be judged according to its standards. For example, a psychologist would be judged against the APS Code of Ethics if called to court to answer an allegation of negligence. Whether or not the psychologist thinks that the guidelines in the Code of Ethics are wrong or inappropriate, it is the majority standard to be applied. I believe that the RPP would be aware of the code of ethics of their own profession.

The following example highlights in practical terms how negligence might apply. A private physiotherapist works in a hospital. He is a bit of a joker and likes to clown around. He has a student on placement. One day he picks up a somewhat heavy briefcase and tosses it at the student. It hits her in the stomach when she failed to catch it. Later he finds out she had her appendix removed the week before and, after being hit by the case, the stitches were re-opened which caused her to bleed internally. Immediately after being hit she was fine, however, she later developed complications when the wound became infected. She spent two weeks in hospital due to the complications and had to repeat a year of her course. Was the therapist negligent?

The outcome is obviously disproportionate to the act. The physiotherapist did not know that she had had the operation (or stitches) and he did not know that the injury would put her in hospital for two weeks. According to the principles of negligence, he did not have to actually foresee the exact consequences of his actions, only that tossing a heavy bag could cause a problem. The fact that the outcome was more serious than expected does not matter. It is not the outcome that determines the level of negligence (although the outcome will determine the size of the damages), it is the foreseeable consequences of the act. So in a case like this, the physiotherapist may be found negligent for that injury. Negligence is not simply the act or the outcome; it is also the circumstances that have led to the outcome.

To consider negligence in more detail, it is important to consider the four main components of negligence (Cohen, 1995). These are:

1. A duty of care.

2. A breach of duty.

3. Causation and proximate cause.

4. Damages.

A duty of care is involved when someone provides a service. That is, anyone providing a professional service has a duty to provide reasonable care. As a helping professional this is implicit in every situation. So if you work with people with medical conditions (for example as an occupational health and safety officer), should you have CPR and first aid training? Would the RPP? If you do a lot of medical work, such as in physiotherapy, I would argue that the reasonably prudent health worker, dealing with a lot of medical conditions, should probably be trained in first aid. However, if you deal with people in other areas of the profession, then there may be valid reasons why you need not be trained in first aid. You need to anticipate what a RPP would do in any given case.

Any professional, when providing a service, has a certain degree of legal responsibility in relation to the welfare and safety of others. One of the best sources of information for those involved in counselling is the book "Risky practices" by Nigel McBride and Michael Tunnecliffe(2001).   It outlines many aspects that need to be understood to minimise risk.

Many professionals do not understand the breadth of the duty of care principle. For example, if you conduct a training course and, during the coffee break, someone asks for a bit of advice, which you then provide. If they then act on that advice, and it fails, you may be sued. Many professionals are surprised to learn that just because they did not get paid, that doesn't mean that they did not have a duty of care. What McBride and Tunnecliffe argue that in certain circumstances you have a duty of care outside the obvious patient-practitioner relationship. The bottom line is that, as a health care professional, there are certain responsibilities connected to the provision of advice for which you may be held accountable under certain circumstances.

The breach of duty is an act, or failure to act, that creates an unreasonable risk of harm. Suppose an architect chooses to provide a service such as creating designs for a new house. The house is designed to function on solar power. The type of roofing is not structurally strong enough to support the solar panels and collapses in the first winter storm causing injury to the new owners. Should the RRP have also consulted a structural engineer? I would have thought so.

Causation and proximate cause relates to the way in which the damage occurred. It is the means of determining blame for damage. This is where the law gets technical. It is where there are complex arguments in court about the degree to which one act is responsible for causing an outcome. The heart of negligence concerns whether the injury resulted from an unreasonable risk of harm that was a reasonably foreseeable consequence of the person's conduct.

It is not the purpose of this book to highlight all areas of risk management. Informed consent, risk to self or others, and other legal issues also arise in relation to the above examples. If, after reading the material in this book, you have further questions, seek advice on managing risk from legal, financial and insurance professionals.

In order to claim damages, a legally recognisable injury or loss must be shown to have occurred. If determined, then that victim can be compensated at your expense. Historically, non-medical areas of the health profession have been relatively safe from negligence claims because those areas tend not to cause physical harm. Failure to make someone better is not necessarily considered to be negligence. It may be incompetence, which can result in Registration Board complaints, but if there was no actual damage, it would be hard for someone to sue. Typically, for this reason, psychologists and counsellors do not get sued very much. Due to problems associated with medication, psychiatrists are subject to negligence claims more frequently than psychologists. However, compared to other medical specialists, psychiatrists are at the lower end of the range of claims. Obstetrics is one of the worst fields for negligence claims as there are greater risks and, due to the young age of the victims, compensation is calculated by reference to losses over a lifetime.

There is a wide variation in how often and how successfully lawsuits are instituted against other professions. In my opinion, there is no such thing as a "safe" profession. Anyone can be sued.

One of the areas of damage which McBride and Tunnecliffe believe has significant implications for counsellors, therapists and other mental health workers is that of financial loss. Consider this simple example. Suppose you are a counsellor teaching someone assertiveness skills on a one-to-one basis. While assertiveness is a relatively simple skill, some clients go to extremes when they first practice the skill. For example, the client starts telling everyone "where to go", which is aggressive, not assertive, behaviour. They then go to work and tell their boss to get stuffed and consequently they get the sack. They are unemployed for over three months and they gradually become depressed to the point where they need hospitalisation. They then sue you for the three months' loss of income and hospital treatment because you should have foreseen that learning assertiveness skills would have caused them to be aggressive with their boss. As you failed to adequately warn and advise against this course of action you may be found to be negligent. While I do not know whether we have had such cases within the mental health professions, the possibility is not that far-fetched.

Risk Management is concerned with how to set yourself up so as not to be sued. Having raised negligence as an issue, I would expect that you are now nervous about the implications for yourself as a professional. There are a handful of approaches open to you. These include; avoiding the risk, accepting the risk, reducing the risk and transferring the risk. Although I offer an introduction to some of these approaches, I would recommend that you read the literature and seek advice related to risk management within your specific profession.

Avoiding the risk is the first approach to risk management. That is, do not do certain types of work. If you are extremely concerned about risk management, you can always cease working, not talk to anyone, and build a bunker (and not leave it). This is an extreme over-statement, but probably the only way to avoid most risks.

A more useful and effective approach is to recognise that there are some areas of practice that carry greater risk. For example, if you work in the area of Family Court disputes, expect to receive hostile responses and to be the subject of complaints to the Registration Board. A Family Court lawyer said to me recently that if you have not had at least three complaints to the legal practitioners' association, you are either new or not doing your job. This is because family breakdown is an emotive business and some people are unreasonable. By recognising the higher risk areas, you can then choose not to work in those areas.

Accepting the risk is the second approach to risk management. This involves analysing the benefits and the problems related to particular types of work, and then making an informed choice. I suspect that most professionals do certain work because it is available to them, rather than consciously choosing to do that work. The more you understand the risks associated with your area of work, the greater the likelihood you will manage them.

In accepting the risk, it is important to realise that it is not only about what you do. Even if you are the best in your profession, it is not necessary for you to have done something wrong for a person to sue you. An aggrieved party only has to believe that you have done something wrong. Even if there is a trial, and you are not held to be responsible, it may still cost you between $20,000 and $50,000 in legal fees to defend yourself (or more if you are a company), unless costs are awarded to you.

Lawyers are increasingly using a shotgun approach to take action. For example, suppose that you modify and run training courses developed by a training organisation. You run the training but it goes badly. A lawyer might sue the people who wrote the material, you as the person who implemented it, and the agency that employed you to implement it. That is, all three parties become part of the lawsuit. The lawyer will then sort out who was actually responsible. You may have to have a lawyer represent you for the next two to ten years before you are held not to be responsible. This may not be fair but, as noted in the introductory sections of this book, the law is not concerned with fairness but with applying rules to a dispute.

Reducing the risk involves being a RPP. Keeping up with current knowledge and training is an important aspect of reducing risk. When the Australian Psychological Society introduced Professional Development points (PD points) I thought it was an unnecessary burden. However, one advantage of having a PD point record is that if a lawyer asks in court: "You were not up-to-date with the training were you?" you can respond: "I have met the requirements of my professional society in Professional Development training; here is my certificate to prove it". Irrespective of your profession, training and staying up-to-date is essential.

You can reduce risk by keeping abreast of the latest changes, including changes to legislation. Workers' compensation is one area in which the legislation seems to change the most. If you work in the area of workers' compensation, you have to determine the current situation or risk providing incorrect information to your clients.

Privacy legislation is another area where many professionals get caught out. If you work for a government department, you will be familiar with the principles of accountability associated with freedom of information (see, for example, the Freedom of Information Act 1982 (Cwlth)). Privacy legislation has recently been extended to the private sector. It has had a huge impact upon the way in which practitioners run their activities. Unfortunately, most professionals do not really understand the implications of the privacy legislation. For example, I was told that one of the first successful cases, which used the National Privacy Principles (Privacy Act 1988 (Cwlth), sch. 3) against a health professional, involved someone seeing a client for only a few sessions. The patient did not pay, so the therapist sent the account to a debt collection agency. The debt collection agency contacted the patient who then complained to the Privacy Commissioner. The Privacy Act 1988 (Cwlth) provides that a person's name and address is confidential information, therefore, the health professional was guilty of breaching the Act. If you do not have a clause in your intake information that allows you to release information for debt collection purposes, then you run the risk of breaching the Act.

Good judgment, based on a reasonable assessment of the situation, is the best way to reduce risk. However, good judgment is a difficult construct to learn, or indeed teach. If you act conservatively you will tend to make good judgments.

In the American literature, a study examined the correlation between the type of qualification and the frequency of being sued. The study compared professionals with different levels of qualifications (for example, bachelor, master's degree, and doctorate). The study found that the more highly qualified the professional, the less likely they were to be sued. A finding such as this is likely to be the case in other professions. The key ingredients in lowering risk include ensuring that you are properly trained, working within your area of expertise, and using good judgment in all that you do.

Supervision, referral and peer review are processes that can help to lower risk. It is important to document the fact that you discussed case details with your colleagues (under the National Privacy Principles you need to ensure that your client has given consent for case discussion). For example, if you are dealing with a suicidal patient, document the steps you have taken to address the risk. I have several friends who are psychiatrists. In this example

I might contact one of them and ask: "I have this person who is really suicidal. I have done the following. What do you reckon?" Their response might be: "That seems an appropriate course of action". I then write in my notes: "Consultation with psychiatrist Joe Blogs, date, and note that the psychiatrist agrees with plan". A five-minute telephone call is all it takes but, if I was ever in a situation where I was being sued, I have improved my position by having input from a psychiatrist. If the matter went to court, a clinical psychologist would be seen to be a suitable professional for dealing with a suicidal person but, unless a medical practitioner addresses the medical issues, the psychologist's position may not be fully defensible. A GP is seen as a generalist who is capable of dealing with minor mental health issues but discussion with a psychiatrist would strengthen their position in a similar manner. Depending on your own profession and expertise, it is important that you do likewise.

As I have stressed, you should document your processes. When asked about how much detail to include in case notes, there are two opposing arguments. If you are going to be sued for negligence, the more detail you have in your notes, the better you can protect yourself if someone tries to sue you. If you write "Referred to GP" in your notes or in your diary on the day you saw a suicidal client, then that information backs up your position – it has the appearance of truth thereby making your arguments seem more plausible. If not documented, you would have to say: "I think I told them that they should talk to their doctor". The lawyer, with an incredulous tone, will bite back with: "Think? You said think? Do you not know for sure? How certain are you?" You respond hesitantly: "90 per cent certain". The lawyer then puts to you: "So, there's a 10 per cent chance you killed this person!" From someone who inadvertently overlooks writing a comment on a file, you could be labelled responsible for killing a client. On the other hand, if someone subpoenas your file for another purpose, such as for the Family Court, the less detail on the file the harder it is for them to cross-examine you.

The timing of the recording of notes is also important. More weight will be given to notes recorded close to the occurrence of the event. If you write your notes while talking to the person, your records would be viewed more positively than if you simply write a summary afterwards (which in turn would be given more weight than a summary written at the end of the day or week). If I am writing a forensic assessment I will take verbatim notes as much as possible. I will also write down my questions and any observed behaviours at the time.

Some professionals tape or digitally record their interviews with clients. Taped rather than handwritten notes would probably carry more weight, but you have to consider whether; (a) it is worth stockpiling thousands of tapes in your cupboard, and (b) whether you can afford the expense of getting them transcribed. Digital records take less space and the material lasts longer (a video cassette or tape lasts for approximately 8 years) so digital records are better in relation to storage, but the same problem exists in relation to the costs of transcription. It is a personal choice for many professionals at this stage, as it is not yet an expected practice except in those directly gathering evidence, for example, police departments (but do check your profession's expectations). For many professionals the decision to record is still a personal choice (except for those, such as police officers, who have an obligation to record evidence), however, check the requirements of your profession in this regard.

If you do record information, be aware that there are certain requirements in relation to privacy and consent. Permission should normally be granted prior to recording. There are also laws in relation to the recording of telecommunications. In addition, there are issues in relation to the question of whether children, especially young children, can give consent. I don't provide an answer to these issues; I merely highlight them so that you can seek the appropriate legal advice.

Recently I was asked whether verbatim notes scrawled out during an interview could be summarised and the original notes of the session destroyed. From a court's perspective, the verbatim notes would be considered to be the evidence with the most weight. From a professional's perspective we do not really care about the evidence; we care about the formulation. Unfortunately, lawyers care about the evidence upon which a formulation is based. If you write notes and later destroy them, be prepared to justify your procedure, and be prepared for vicious treatment in court. I have also been advised that there are potentially serious legal implications in relation to the destruction of evidence. This creates an interesting situation with technology as used by large government departments. Many departments now require their workers to upload case notes directly to a central recording system. This may lower the contemporaneousness of the writing process.

There are other ways of reducing risk and managing consent. For example, I provide my clients with written or verbal agreements about what to expect. It is all about informed consent. By law, a court may order a client to attend upon certain professionals (for example, a forensic accountant for a review of matters in relation to a Family Court case). However, I would still take the time to explain to a client about confidentiality and the fact that everything they tell me may end up in a report.

To manage the consent process, I send all new clients a letter, together with a copy of the Privacy Principles I have developed for my practice, which is then signed and placed on the file.

The transfer of risk is an important consideration. Assuming, after evaluating the risks within your practice, you continue to work as a professional. What do you do about the risk? Insurance allows you to transfer the largest proportion of risk to somebody else. There may be limits to what the insurance will cover so you need to read your policy carefully. However, if you are successfully sued, and you are insured, you will not be liable for the cost. If you are not insured, you may risk losing your assets (such as your house or car).

The downside is that insurance is expensive. A newspaper article I reviewed when writing the first edition of this book (West Australian, 14 June, 2003) noted that a non-procedural GP paid $7,200 for their annual insurance; neurosurgeons paid $45,500; while the fee for medical obstetrics was $97,000. Psychologists complained because our insurance was costing nearly $700 in that year! The amounts change from year to year but the comparative differences remain the same.

When considering insurance coverage, most policies are "date of claim" policies. This means that if you see a client in 2009, and the patient later claims that you did something negligent but they do not file a claim until March 2012, it is the 2012, not the 2009, policy that applies.

Upon retirement, it is important to ensure that you have sufficient insurance coverage into the future. Roll-on cover is generally included when someone retires but what happens if someone returns to paid employment from private practice? How long does the roll-on last? When managing your risk, these are the questions you need to ask your financial advisor and insurance broker.

There are financial strategies that can be used to minimise risk. Some accountants now advise the transfer of assets into a partner's name because it is an individual, not a couple, who could be sued. If your partner is not likely to be sued, and they will remain with you in the future, it may be advantageous to transfer your assets into their name. Options include trusts, asset transfers, and so on. Seek appropriate financial advice about this type of strategy.

A colleague raised an interesting consequence relating to being insured and settling out of court. Years ago a client raised a claim of negligence against the colleague. A small out of court settlement was made. Since that time the practitioner has not been able to get any insurance! Settling at one point has resulted in other insurers being unwilling to cover that practitioner. The lesson here is to be very careful about what you agree to when dealing with insurance companies.

Key Points

- Negligence is "an unintentional fault, or carelessness resulting in injury. It deals with avoidable incidents which should have been anticipated and prevented by taking reasonable precautions" (Cohen, 1995).

- When appearing in court, the worst position to be in is when your own livelihood is on the line. Negligence claims arise when you have either done something wrong or someone believes that you have.

- As you will be judged against the theoretical "reasonably prudent professional", ensure that your manner of practicing matches the professional standard by being evidence-based, mainstream, careful, and conservative.

- Following codes of ethics, understanding and maintaining policies and procedures, and staying within professional practice standards are all safeguards against negligence claims

- Insurance against malpractice and other types of liability is essential. However, ensure that you understand the policy and how it applies in special cases (for example, in retirement).

- Should you be required to defend yourself, accurate and detailed records are worth their weight in gold.

- Prior to settling even small claims out of court, discuss the implications of that settlement with a legal practitioner or insurance expert.

3

Writing Reports for Court

The Nature of Report Writing

After receiving a lawyer's request for evidence, your information has to be put together in a manner that is useful to the court. Sometimes your evidence may be given verbally, however, for reasons that will become evident later, a written report is the format generally required. Depending on the initial brief, the report may be sent directly to the court, sworn as an affidavit, or sent to the briefing lawyer. The briefing lawyer will advise you in relation to their requirements.

Anyone who has studied human behaviour knows that presentation is everything. How you structure your report, the words used to describe things, and the order in which the information is presented, all impact on how the report will be perceived. It is critical that you think about the structure of your report. The following represents some of the things you should consider.

It is critical that any report meets the standards and expectations of your profession, including ethical requirements, and is written in accordance with codes of professional conduct.

KISS Principle

The "KISS" principle means "Keep It Simple, Sweetheart" (or for the more negatively inclined, "Keep It Simple, Stupid"). Very early in my career a barrister friend said: "Write your reports like the lawyers and judges are ignorant of the topic because they probably are". This was an extremely blunt way of putting it but I accepted her underlying message. When you write your report, unless the lawyers are specialists who work in the field and are very familiar with the literature, they will not understand any but the simplest of the profession's terminology. I avoid using jargon as much as possible. The safest assumption to make is that the reader has no previous knowledge of your area of expertise. (A small number of lawyers or barristers might have dual degrees (after practicing in a particular area), and therefore have extensive expertise. Fortunately, they are in the minority.

Consider the following example. What is domestic violence? Does it include slapping your partner in the face during a fight? Or burning your partner's clothes if you disagree? Or smashing every piece of furniture with a baseball bat? Or taking your partner into the bush at gunpoint and raping her? I would argue that all of these scenarios could be defined as domestic violence. The critical question is; would it help a judge in the Family Court to say that domestic violence existed in a relationship? The alternative is to say the following: "This person has a set of rigid beliefs which he enforces in a demeaning way"; "This person has a temper problem which results in sudden violence"; or "This person is likely to act out, stalk and then become violent when rejected". By using a description of the behaviour, rather than simply using jargon like "domestic violence", the court is in a much better position to make a finding.

Similarly, an accountant who has a model based on "theoretical entities", or an engineer who cites "stress tolerance ratios", runs a serious risk of being sorely misunderstood. Your profession may understand the meaning, but a court needs the information in a way that can be understood.

At the other end of the scale, I have experienced problems when I have kept the language too simple. I have ended up in an argument about the definition of "feral children" in a court report. The term described the situation perfectly, but I ended up debating what I actually meant because the words were too colloquial and seeming to be too casual in my approach.

It is important to be careful about how emotive you get. In one of my reports I used the description: "Worst case I had seen for some time". During the trial, a QC hammered me for ages about the basis for the description. While I still believe that it was a worst case, the judge decided that I had been emotive in my response and believed that I had not liked the client. Much of my evidence was then discarded. The safest path is to understate rather than over-emphasise the point (that is, avoid the emotive or the extreme).

I try to keep the language common and err towards being simplistic. On numerous occasions I have been asked by lawyers to explain aspects of the medical or psychological reports of other professionals because the lawyers did not understand what had been written. Having read those reports, I can understand the lawyers' frustrations as I too had trouble following the reports. If you are talking to different people, and lawyers are different people, use a narrative they can understand.

It is important, however, that you do not become so vague that you lose all meaning. You need to be as precise as possible. One of the worst complaints about some professionals' reports is that the reports tend to cover too many bases. For example, the reports say: "If this, then that, maybe this", and so on. Medically trained specialists, such as psychiatrists, will often review a patient and say: "This is the way it is", which is easier for the court. The court likes us to have an opinion, but we have got to be careful to find a balance between covering options conservatively, and not having an opinion. It is critical that you make sure that you have a view, but that you also show the logic leading to that view.

One of the most useful strategies when writing a report is to list the main options and then remove those that are unlikely. By doing this you are demonstrating to the court your process of reasoning, something that is highly regarded by lawyers. I will explain more about this point later.

Citing Professional Literature

A concern held by some professionals is in relation to whether or not literature should be cited in a court report. In Western Australia this argument became quite heated because one psychologist would often provide reports with up to 60 references. That person would then argue that everyone else, in not citing literature, was wrong and that only their own approach was correct. In my opinion judges do not get any value from lists of references, nor would they seek out the literature to read the material, so there seems to be no real point in including them. In other words, do not cite references unless you use them for good reason.

Our differing opinions resulted in a clash during a trial. On that occasion our opinions in relation to literature citations came before the court. I had directly assessed a family, and the other psychologist had given a second opinion on my report. The other psychologist criticised, among other things, the lack of references in my report. During my evidence, I took the opportunity to seek the judge's opinion whether or not references should be cited. When asked a question about the literature I commented to the effect that: "It would be helpful to the profession if we had some guidance as to how much referencing to the professional literature we should include in our report". In his summing up, Judge Barlow stated:

Because of the nature of psychology, more likely than not there will forever be debates and disagreements between psychologists in relation to human behaviour. Generally I do not think a court is the appropriate forum for that debate. There may be cases where a witness who purports to be an expert puts forward a view or opinion based on a theory or methodology, but is yet to gain general acceptance, or alternatively a theory or model which is yet to be completely discredited. Obviously, in such a case it would be appropriate for the court to hear evidence relevant to the credibility of the theory or methodology. However, in cases which do not fall in that category it is unlikely that detailed referencing to the psychological studies will be of any, or at least of any significant, assistance to a trial judge.

This makes sense. A judge is not going to seek the professional literature and review our journal articles. We are in court to give expert evidence. On the basis of this ruling I would argue that you only need to cite significant or controversial references and, if you are quoting from test manuals, cite that information.

However, the guidelines for expert evidence in the Family Court of Australia, and codes of conduct in various states, require that an expert must explain the reasons for their decision. Rule 15.63 of the Family Law Rules 2004 (Cwlth) states: "An expert's report must ... include the following in support of the expert witness's conclusions: ... (ii) the literature or other material used in making the report". This requirement extends to the need for a well-considered rationale, based on the professional literature. Hence, many professionals may need to go back to the library to ensure that they are well versed in the material upon which they are basing their decisions.

I would argue that if you are offering an expert opinion, you should integrate a wide body of knowledge and not rely upon discrete journal articles. It is critical to realise the difference between citing literature and knowing the literature. An effective expert is familiar with a wide cross-section of the literature and will be able to give examples of landmark studies if necessary. The point is that you do not, when preparing a report, have to cite all of the articles you have ever read, but you must cite any material specifically used.

Finally, there is another issue with respect to referencing. In Western Australia I have seen some colleagues use psychological tests with computer scoring systems and subsequently include verbatim chunks of the computer interpretations in their reports. I never use a computer-generated interpretation in court because it is not my opinion but a computer's opinion. I always score the protocol and offer my opinion of what the test means in my own words. In the medical sector, it is similar to the difference between someone relying on a radiologist's report of a scan and personally looking at the scan results and offering an opinion. The first is another's expertise; the second relies on your own expertise. Everyone can look at the raw data, but the expert has the experience and knowledge to offer an opinion about what the data actually means. Therefore, it is critical to reference sources of material that are not your own opinions.

The "Ultimate Issue"

During a trial, the judge sits in court listening to lawyers asking questions of witnesses or otherwise droning on for hours. The judge does not appear to do much other than make the occasional comment about principles of law, guide the process, and to stay awake while they gather information upon which to base their decision. Once all the evidence has been received, the judge's (if there is no jury) one bit of excitement is to hand down a finding. The judge has formed a view about all of the information and gets the chance to say: "Guilty for these reasons"; "Not guilty"; or "I will make this decision or recommend this much compensation". This is the determination of the ultimate issue. It is the prerogative of the judge alone to make the ultimate judgment. Indeed, I would say that addressing the ultimate issue is required of the judge. Although the individual law varies in the expectation placed upon the judge to address the ultimate issue, being respectful of their role is critical to good evidence.

An understanding of the concept of the ultimate issue is critical as it draws the line between the point at which professionals should finish their arguments and where the judge's exclusive role begins. The most common mistake made by people inexperienced with the court is that they overstep the mark and try to take over the judge's role. For example, when it comes time for the trial, if I am asked: "Where do you think the children should live in this family court matter?" I would respond: "I provided my opinions to the court in a report based on the evidence I had. At this time the trial has been going for three days, the judge has information available to him or her which I am not privy too, therefore residence is now their decision and my views no longer matter." Usually the judge starts nodding in agreement and says to the lawyer: "Yes, Dr Watts is right", which quickly stops the lawyer from following that line of questioning. It is respectful to the court to let the judge have his or her role. Even if you are asked to explain further, adhering to this approach shows the judge respect. The judge does not want a social worker to come into court and say where the children should live; or an accountant say how property should be divided (in a Family Court dispute); or a psychologist say whether an accused is guilty! It is the judge's job, and their job alone, to make those findings.

The approach to take when you write your report is to lead the judge to reach a logical conclusion from your report. If you are writing a pre-sentence report, you should not say whether or not the sentence should be one of imprisonment, or how long the sentence should be. However, you can outline the factors indicating whether the person should get a custodial sentence (such as, suicide risk in custody, institutionalisation, vulnerability, impact on rehabilitation, or risk to the community). For example, I once wrote: "This man is from the Kimberley Region of Western Australia. He has never been outside of that region. The charges he is involved in are serious but bringing him to Perth will be harder on him than it would be on a person who normally lives in Perth. I understand the court has various considerations to make in such a case, but in terms of this man's psychological needs, the sooner he can be returned to his community the better he will cope." I have not told the judge what to do but hopefully I have shown him or her a logical possibility.

Similarly, where there is a conflict in accounting practices before a court, the savvy accountant is capable of saying: "I have indicated the facts upon which I calculated my conclusions, his or her honour has had access to facts which I am not necessarily aware of. Unless those facts are put to me, I cannot add to my opinion ...".

In 2002, I contacted the then Chief Judge of the Western Australian District Court to see if he could offer a brief comment on what constitutes good evidence from psychological witnesses. Chief Judge Hammond kindly asked Judge Wisbey to prepare a paper which, with permission from Judge Wisbey, I included as an appendix to the first edition of this book (and therefore include it in this edition). Although the paper relates specifically to evidence of psychological issues, it will have application to other types of expert witnesses. Judge Wisbey had this to say about the ultimate issue:

A psychologist in a personal injury case or a criminal proceeding can give evidence that he or she carried out an examination or testing of a person, and that the testing did or did not reveal any abnormality in the person tested. He or she cannot express an opinion that the tested person is genuine or malingering. The opinion must not extend to usurping the function of the trial judge in reaching the ultimate conclusion as to whether the person is truthful. That opinion is not admissible as the court is well able and required to draw the appropriate conclusion from the evidence presented.

Another way to conceptualise your role in court is to link the ultimate issue to your evidence base. An expression I find useful is: "From a psychological perspective ...". The advantage of this expression is that you are telling the court that you are only one part of the evidence picture. It acknowledges the limitations of the evidence. You are a psychologist (or medical specialist, or engineer etc.) giving psychological (or medical, or engineering etc.) evidence and you do not have all the facts. Never assume that you will ever have all of the facts.

This discussion on the ultimate issue rule may seem like splitting hairs but the subtlety is critical. Following the principle is both a demonstration of your respect for the court, and an acknowledgement of the limits of your evidence. I found it much less stressful when I realised that the court made the decisions; I only assist the court. I was recently involved in a case before the State Administrative Tribunal (SAT) in Western Australia in which the Member said: "Doctor Watts gave his evidence impressively". The only reason I think I was impressive in that case was my understanding of the clear boundary between my role and that of the SAT Member.

Confidentiality

Many practitioners provide treatment on the assumption that the confidentiality they value with their clients is protected in the legal arena. Unfortunately, this is generally not the case. The Australian Psychological Society's Code of Ethics states: "No privilege in Common Law protects communications between a psychologist and a client and because courts can scrutinise documents and files, all consultations and discussions should be recorded" (APS, 2007). My enquiries suggest that this also applies to other professions – even medical doctors and the clergy have difficulty claiming confidentiality over their information.

The law works on the assumption that evidence can be collected and used in court. As explained in the introduction to this book, the government and the judiciary are separate and the High Court's decisions must be accepted by everyone, even governments. Therefore, how would the court function if individual professionals all chose to keep their information privileged?

Once a matter is before the court, some professionals think that writing "confidential" on a report will protect it from public discussion. This is not the case. When you write something, all the lawyers involved need copies of the reports so they can prepare their cases. A person needs to be able to read what was said about them if they are to defend it in court (it is a fundamental right that you should have access to material relevant to the action against you). I work on the assumption that any report sent to the court will be handed around like birthday cake at a children's party. Everyone gets some. In court the parties likely to see the report include the judge, the lawyers or barristers for the parties, the individuals involved, and all other incidental participants in the process. You need to write your report knowing that your client and other people will read it.

Sometimes you may be unlucky enough to be involved in a case where there are really nasty dynamics with potentially fatal consequences. For example, I was involved in a case in which a man had a history of violence and a current major depression, perceived his children as property, had recently separated from his wife, had suicidal ideation involving himself and homicidal ideation involving the children. This was the profile of a man who could drive to the bush and then gas both himself and his children. I wrote the required report but I telephoned the judge's associate to seek advice about how best to manage the process. I was told to provide a covering letter to the report and include the comment: "In my opinion this person is high risk. I recommend this report should not be released until some safeguards are put in place". While it was an unusual step, the court did not release the report until the day of the hearing so as to protect the children. Note, however, the man still had a right to, and did, read the report. While this may be an exceptional circumstance, it is helpful to know that there are options for dealing with difficult situations. To find out how to minimise risks, either talk to the lawyers involved in the case, or to other professionals experienced in the area.

As a matter of professional courtesy, and as required by the ethical guidelines of some professions, if confidential information must be disclosed in court, and the client is not party to the legal proceedings, the client should be advised of the time and date of the trial. This means that if a professional sees a couple for family therapy before separation, and subsequently one of them appears in court on an unrelated matter (for example, a workers' compensation matter), this issue may arise. If a lawyer subpoenas your file and asks you to attend court, you are obliged to notify the other party of the time and place you are going to give evidence. You may have a professional obligation to notify them. I am unaware of whether this is included in the ethical guidelines of other professions but, at a minimum, it does represent professional courtesy. The extent of disclosure becomes difficult as you balance the confidentiality requirements prescribed by your profession's ethical guidelines and the National Privacy Principles on the one hand, and legal requirements for disclosure on the other hand.

The issues are simplified by the use of what is called informed consent. It is important that before you provide a service to someone they know what you are doing. The use of a consent letter allows the client to understand the strengths and limitations of your service. They can then choose whether or not to participate.

The same applies to the release of information. If a person signs an authorisation for the release of privacy information, it helps to establish a paper trail so that if there are repercussions flowing from the release of information you can defend yourself. If a lawyer requests a report, it is good practice to ensure that the client signs a release so that the report can be sent. In many cases the lawyer will provide a signed release. If not, ensure that you get one. The only exceptions to this are in cases where legislation compels the release of information, where there are mandatory reporting requirements of abuse, or with certain aspects of the workers' compensation system (for example, funding based on a requirement to provide regular treatment reports). This is where knowledge of the law applicable in your jurisdiction is critical. Even if a person requests a report, they may not understand how that report is going to be used, who it will be released to, or how they can get a copy.

Similarly, when I first started doing court assessments, my office received a lot of phone calls from people complaining that they did not know what was going on after the report was released. A particularly effective way of managing this situation is to include "notes to the parties" at the beginning or end of each report. For example, in the Family Court I include the new rules that outline the process for asking a question of an expert, after offering some general directions. The following represents my current statement:

If you have any concerns with the report, discuss them with your legal representative. If you do not have your own lawyer, either seek independent legal advice or write to the Separate Representative outlining your concerns.

Please do not make telephone contact with me or my office after the report has been released. Any communication must be in writing (as outlined below), otherwise my position of independence may be jeopardised.

Under Rule 15.65 of the Family Law Rules (2004) [sic. Family Law Rules 2004 (Cwlth)] it states that you may ask questions about an expert's report. However:

Questions must be in writing and can only be put once.

I. It must be within 21 days from when you received the report.

II. Questions can only be for the purpose of clarifying the report.

III. The questions must not be vexatious or oppressive, or require the expert to undertake an unreasonable amount of work.

IV. You must give a copy of any questions to each other party.

V. A single expert witness's reasonable fees and expenses incurred in answering any questions are to be paid by the party ASKING the questions (my rates are based on the APS schedule of fees).

A single expert witness is not required to answer any questions until the fees and expenses for answering them are paid or secured.

The use of this statement does not stop the impulsive, brain-damaged, drug-using client from ringing up, but the more intelligent ones will read it and then use the appropriate channels because they now know what is expected of them. This statement could be adapted easily to reports produced by other professionals.

Credibility

To be successful in court, it is important that you manage the credibility of your evidence. It is essential to ensure that you are knowledgeable and correct. Getting things wrong, using outdated techniques or information, and saying things that are not technically sound are likely to cause you problems in court. As I stated earlier, many lawyers know nothing about your area of practice. However, some may have received training in a non-legal area (such as, accounting, medicine, engineering, or psychology) before becoming lawyers. Similarly, just because the lawyer may not understand your area of practice, it does not mean that they will not get a specialist to provide a second opinion review.

With respect to credibility, it is important to remember that most judges have been around for years. They start out as lawyers and then become barristers. They may become a Senior or Queen's Counsel, and then they are finally appointed as a judge. By this time they have been around for many years. This may be your first professional report for any particular court, but the judge has been reading reports for years. For example, I have produced over 500 reports as a court-appointed expert in the Family Court. There are only about a dozen Family Court judges and magistrates in the WA court, which means that by the time they see your first report, they will have read on average thirty-five of my reports. For better or worse, I will have in part set the standard of what they expect in a psychologist's report.

Law loves precedent. Precedent means that a decision made in one case will become the standard in the next case until it is challenged at a higher level. From a witness's perspective, it is important to be very careful with what you do in each situation, as it may become the precedent in another situation. In the absence of foresight, what you do can come back to haunt you. For example, when I studied at university I majored in psychology with a minor in indigenous Australian anthropology. I subsequently worked in the area of juvenile justice where I had to assess a number of indigenous individuals in a variety of contexts. Recently, I received a request to be a court expert in a case in which an indigenous father had murdered a white mother. The case was a custody dispute between the indigenous and caucasian grandparents of the children (who had lost a mother and had a father in prison). The appointment as a court expert included a clause that there was to be a cultural adviser appointed to advise me of indigenous issues. I have no problem working with a cultural advisor, and I am not arrogant enough to think I know everything about the indigenous population. My concern was in relation to the precedent that this would set. When I found out about that clause, I refused to do the assessment. If I had carried out the assessment with a cultural adviser, this could have been used against me in future cases in any court in which I needed to give evidence on indigenous issues. The lawyer could say: "You needed a cultural adviser in that particular case in the Family Court; surely that means you are not qualified to provide opinions about indigenous people in this court?"

I refused to work with the adviser, not because I thought such a professional would not be beneficial, but because I did not want to get locked into a precedent that said I needed assistance to assess indigenous clients. The irony in this case was that it was the Aboriginal Legal Service of Western Australia's family law section arguing that I needed a cultural adviser (an organisation for which, at the time, I was completing one or two pre-sentence reports a month for their criminal law section). I believe the lawyer was just playing a legal game to help her client, but had I fallen for the trap it could have had a tremendous impact on my future ability to give evidence in court.

You should always remember that you are only as good as your last report. Years ago, one of my colleagues wrote in a juvenile offender presentence report for the President of the Children's Court: "This young man shows no characteristics of a repeat sex offender and is not likely to sex offend again", but within two weeks of sentencing he hadcommitted a horrendous sex offence. This psychologist never worked again in the Children's Court. The reason why the psychologist could not work again is best highlighted in a simple example. I had given evidence in a Family Court trial in relation to a particularly messy case. Immediately after the case concluded, I drove to my office, which is just ten minutes away from the court. As I walked into the office the phone rang. A different lawyer told me how well I had done in court that morning. The moral of the story is that the legal profession is relatively small, particularly within specialist areas, and lawyers network with one another. If you do a good job, it generates lots of work. If you do a bad job, it will be used against you.

It may sound obsessive, but I keep a record of my case involvement because it helps to support my credibility. To be able to say: "I have been appointed as a court expert in 500 Family Court cases" is a strong line to use. To say: "I have given evidence in lots of cases" seems to lose something. Add the statistical record to a string of credibility statements such as, "I've got a Doctor of Philosophy and a Master of Clinical Psychology. I have been working as a professional for 19 years, and I have seen 500 families in the Family Court as court expert" and it puts me in a credible position. Suppose the other party relies on a new graduate who has just finished a Master's degree, is provisionally registered and has completed their first Family Court case. Upon whom will the court put the most weight of evidence? I will be much more credible from the start. The trial process may lead the court to eventually decide that I am a blithering idiot, or factually did not have enough information, while the new graduate could be seen as wonderfully sensible – but my experience and qualifications will give me a head start.

When I run training seminars on giving evidence in court, new graduates frequently ask me what they can do to be credible in court. The short answer is to get older! Seriously, experience is essential so time will improve your credibility. However, if you do not have the experience then you have to rely upon qualifications and study as your strengths.

At the other end of the scale, an interesting recent experience I had in the witness box followed a presentation I had given to lawyers. It also coincided with the release of my book "Shared care or divided lives?". The first lawyer cited sections from the seminar, while the second lawyer read sections of my book to me, and both were getting me to agree with myself! Anything you write, publish or say publicly may potentially be material for lawyers to use with you.

Even with a good qualification and solid experience base, lawyers will play games to challenge your credibility. One technique they can use is a line of questioning that discounts your experience. Consider the following line of questioning: "How many times have you been the court expert in the Family Court?", to which I would respond: "About 500". They then follow up with: "And in how many cases have you assessed someone who is an indigenous Australian?" Suspicious of where they are taking me I respond: "Probably about 80 of those cases". Then the crunch question: "How many cases have you assessed where an indigenous father has killed a white mother?" I then have to answer: "Well, this is my second case". In scoffing tones the lawyer then queries: "And you call yourself an expert?" If I am quick I chip in: "But the principles of best interest of children are not an indigenous issue but rests on general principles of developmental psychology, of which I have immense experience". They were taking my evidence from the general to the specific; I had bring it back to the general principles.

Key Points

- A well-written report is your safeguard against going to court. It will minimise the time you are actually in court, and it will be the backbone of your defence once in the witness box.

- You should address your comments using simple language, written to the level of an intelligent, tertiary educated person who knows nothing about the topic.

- When using simple language, do not become too colloquial or imprecise. It is important for your descriptions to be clear.

- Emotional descriptions, emotional reactions, and personal feelings do not have a place in an evidence-based system.

- Explain the process for reaching the conclusion, because revealing your logic is helpful to the court. Likewise, the process of presenting several key alternative possible explanations for the evidence, and explaining why they are not likely, is well regarded by the legal profession.

- A judge is unlikely to read the professional literature cited in the report (although lawyers might). Consequently, extensive citing of professional literature is probably of little or no use to the judge.

- You must, however, cite key literature, literature that has been directly quoted, controversial literature, and material from manuals, etc.

- Even though you might not cite the literature, it is critical that you understand the literature. An expert must understand what the professional literature says about the issue.

- The ultimate issue is the issue that the court has been convened to determine.

- The reports considered to be the best are those written by professionals who understand the ultimate issue. The report gives the judge all of the information they need to make the decision, but stops short of taking over the judge's responsibility.

- If you understand that you are providing just another piece of information for the judge, it makes the task of preparing the report easier. The alternative is to think that the case is all based upon your report, which creates a situation in which you will overstep your role.

- Courts generally have the power to override confidentiality that normally exists between professionals and their clients. It is important to get legal advice when there are questions relating to the confidentiality of records.

- The communications between the briefing lawyer and a professional may be protected under law. Therefore, be careful when releasing those communications.

- Reports written for court, with very few exceptions, will be seen by all parties involved in the court process (once the matter progresses to trial). Write the report on the assumption that all parties will see the report.

- Writing "confidential" or "for the judge's eyes only" on a report will not necessarily prevent the report from being seen by others.

- It is important that your clients understand their rights and the limits of confidentiality. This should be explained either verbally or in writing, depending on the circumstances.

- Credibility is essential for your survival in court. It is built gradually but may be lost quickly as you are only as good as your last report.

- It important to consider the future implications of decisions made now. Lawyers remember precedents and what you did in one case may come back to haunt you in another.

- Your credibility is to be cherished and protected by being careful, honest, sensible, and thoughtful.

Rules of Report Writing

Rule 1 – Write to the Audience

When we get down to the nuts and bolts of writing good reports there are some basic rules. The first rule is that you have to write to your target audience. You have to get the information to the people for whom you are writing. Ultimately, in a report for court, the judge is your target audience. Who is the person least likely to actually read a report in most areas of law, apart from pre-sentence reports? The judge. Most matters settle, so the ultimate audience does not actually read the report.

The lawyers preparing the case are the ones who are

going to read the report the most. Lawyers want you to be very precise and say exactly what should happen, whereas if you write a report for a judge you should not tell the judge what to do. Therefore, what lawyers need, and what the judge wants, will conflict in some ways. There may also be a second opinion reviewer of the report. In this day and age lawyers who do not understand your report will send it to somebody else who does. In this way you may be writing for three levels of audience; the judge, the lawyers, and others.

The judge will not care about statistics. They will not care about the tests used or the scores obtained, but they will care about what it means. If you used a particular theory or model, it will not mean anything to the judge or lawyers, but it will mean a lot to a second opinion reviewer. For example, I almost never put details of test results in the body of my reports; I add them as an appendix because the judge and the lawyers will not understand it. I therefore put as much as can be understood in the body of the report, and then put the rest of the material at the end so that it is available to read.

Rule 2 – Answer the Question

The second rule of report writing is to answer the question being asked. How do you know what is going to be asked? It may be explicit in that there could be a term of reference or court order (this will be discussed in more detail later). Most professionals are conditioned like Pavlov's dogs. In this famous psychological experiment it was noticed that dogs salivated on the sound of food arriving (and later on the sound of a ringing bell) even before the food was present. The response was provoked by the stimulus. The professional does the same thing – the request for a report arrives, so the professional replies without questioning whether or not they should do so. They are conditioned to see the letter and then write the report.

I would argue that the first thing you should do is telephone the solicitor and find out whether a report is necessary. If there is doubt (such as, whether you are a suitable person to write the report, or whether it will jeopardise your relationship with your client) then explaining that to the lawyer may help you to get out of providing a report. Lawyers are not interested in paying you to write a report that they do not want or need. Similarly, if it is not clear what the lawyers want, clarify their needs before you write the report. Most professionals, unless they work in the legal area a lot, are too scared to telephone a lawyer. I contact lawyers routinely. Contacting the lawyer enables you to get clarification before you start.

I would like to emphasise one key point; a good report tells a story. A factual story, but a story nonetheless. If the report is written really well, it is not just a collection of facts – the situation should clearly come to life. You should be able to get a sense of what the person or situation is really like. If you read a report and get a sense of what a person is like, then you have done a good job. A simple way to test your report is to ask someone (for example, if you have an intelligent, educated partner who knows nothing about your work topic), to read your report to see whether they can make sense of it. They do not need to be trained within your profession to understand a report written for court. In fact I would argue the opposite. If you have to be professionally trained to follow the line of argument in your report, you have written a university report, not a court report.

Rule 3 – Base the Report on Evidence

The third rule in report writing is that the report has to be evidence-based. Facts are absolutely critical. The better you can illustrate the basis of your report (what you have directly seen, heard and experienced), and the clearer you are about the other material you have relied upon, the better your report will stand up in court. If you do not have facts, then your report is going to be blown to pieces during cross-examination.

An electrical engineer from New South Wales, David Burger, shared an example of the way in which practical examples of difficult concepts help to get evidence across in a case. The case, in the Supreme Court, concerned a dispute between Optus and the Tax Office over the sales tax treatment of optical fibre. It involved an amount of around $70M in tax (immediately prior to the introduction of the GST). The case hinged upon the disparity between ordinary copper phone cables (tax free) and optical cables (22% tax) – identical to install, and functionally similar. David was the expert witness for Optus. He wrote a report about the two products being functionally similar but said: "It was when I took everyone to [the] site to see optical and copper cables side by side that convinced the players that there was no pragmatic difference between the two". This example illustrates that it is important to get complex facts into simple understanding.

As a professional, not only do you need to get abstract concepts into simple terms, but the court is also interested in scientific certainty. We are offering information at a professional level. We are not crystal ball gazing or speculating. Your findings are logical conclusions based upon the evidence. A professional witness is a type of scientist – medical science, social science, engineering science, and so on. If you are not a scientist, you are a witness of fact. If you do not have scientific certainty about your findings, and you cannot explain where your conclusion has come from, then you are just offering your opinion (lay opinion), which is not of any use to the court.

If you ask lawyers about the biggest problem with professional evidence they will often say that we do not argue the link between fact and opinion. There is a collection of facts relating to what we have done, and then we have an opinion, but they cannot understand how we arrived at that opinion. Being able to justify your opinions is the skill and the art which will save your butt in court. If you can argue why you have reached that opinion, how that fact pattern results in the opinion in your report, when you go to court you will have an easier time. If you cannot, then you create problems for yourself.

Key Points

- A report has to be written to cover multiple levels of readership but, ultimately, it has to be written for the judge. The carefully crafted report will, however, assist all readers.

- The report must answer the question being asked or it will not be of benefit to those who need it.

- Court is an evidence-based system requiring an evidence-based report. Professional opinions are based on facts and derived from science.

The Structure of Reports

The actual process of writing a report is something that is taught at university. I find, however, that the academic approach teaches you how to write reports for others within the profession, or in the general health area, but not for the legal arena. This section addresses the issue of how to write a report for court. Keeping in mind the general principles already discussed, the next step is the way in which information should be structured. There is no one perfect structure to a court report, but certain elements should be included.

Addressed to whom?

Reports can be addressed to judges or magistrates by name or title, or they can be addressed to lawyers. What you need to do is to find out from the briefing lawyer what the normal protocol is. If you do not write many reports, find out to whom you should send the report, because there are different rules in different circumstances. If the Family Court appointed you as a single expert, you have to file the report with the Court. The covering letter is addressed to the Senior Records Clerk, and the report is addressed to the Principal Registrar. There are very clear instructions. However, if the parties jointly appoint you in the Family Court, you have to release the report simultaneously to both parties rather than to the court. If you produce an assessment for one or other parent, the report should be sent to the lawyer (not to the court or the parties).

If you are not a court expert, you should address your report to the lawyers (unless requested by the court to do something different). Some people will send the report to the court, and include a covering letter to the lawyer. You need to find out from the person who briefed you what their protocol is.

Headings

I believe that it is important to have sections in your report, regardless of your subject area. The bigger the report, the more sections with headings you'll need. Too many headings will disjoint a report. There needs to be enough headings to separate the topics into important sections, but do not overdo it as it kills the flow of the report.

Headings have a really important purpose in that they separate your background data from your facts and from your opinion. At a minimum, for a short report (for example, if you are just treating someone and providing a treatment report) you might only have three headings. You might have a couple of paragraphs in which you outline why you have seen the person, why you have written the report, what you saw in the treatment, and then you will have a heading for an opinion or a conclusion. A comprehensive report can have many headings.

One heading to pay attention to is the title of the report. I always have a title on my reports and I try not to use a generic name like "Psychological Report". I try to use "Treatment Report"; "Pre-Sentence Psychological Report"; etc. In this way I already set the expectation. If I called the report a "Treatment Psychological Report" then when I am being cross-examined, the lawyer could say: "You did not do an independent forensic assessment". I can then say: "If you look at the title you can see it is called a Treatment Report". I do not do it in a derogatory way, but merely refer the lawyer back to the information base.

Date

While dating a report seems obvious, from time to time I have been asked to make modifications to a report. It becomes critical to ensure that altered copies are correctly dated so that, when asked to admit a report into evidence in court, the corrected report is the basis of your evidence. The date is the most obvious identifying feature for reports that have been changed.

From the point of view of ethics and impartiality, should you change your report at the request of a lawyer? By writing a report that the lawyer wants, you are assured of getting repeat business. The cost associated with that is that you are no longer an impartial writer. By being a hired gun or ghost writer for the lawyer, you are doing a disservice to both the court and the profession. Once you have finished a report, it is critical to consider carefully the implications before changing the report.

In my opinion, the critical variable in deciding whether to change a report is the nature of the change. If I change my opinion at the request of the lawyer, I am being unethical. It is not uncommon, however, for a lawyer to ask for a paragraph to be deleted or a sentence changed. One of the first issues to sort out is why they want the change made. If it is because you have factual errors (for example, a date, name or place is wrong) you should change it. Similarly, typographical errors or omissions may be identified and, if significant, should be changed. If you have included something, which under the rules of evidence is not admissible, your forensic logic will be flawed. Therefore, it may be legally appropriate to remove it. On the other hand, I would never change my opinion on the basis of a request. Ethically, an opinion should neither be negotiable nor should it be for sale. If you are provided with new information that changes your opinion, it is a different matter. However, I would recommend that you do not actually change your original report but provide a supplementary or updated report outlining the new information and explaining the reason for your change of opinion.

In cases where the request is related to wording, rules of evidence, or other factors not obvious to me, then I consider the request on the merits of the individual situation. Some simple examples, highlighting the decision-making process, are as follows. I wrote a report for a lady involved in a negligence claim after her husband was killed. I described her as "grieving". The solicitor wanted me to explain whether it was normal grief (which cannot be compensated) or whether the grief was pathological in some way. The request seemed reasonable so I elaborated on the issue in a supplementary report. In another case, when writing a pre-sentence report, I went into a lot of detail about the offender's account to me of an offence. The lawyer explained to me that at the trial the judge made a different finding about the facts of the crime. He asked me to remove the details of the offence as recounted. I agreed, but only on the basis that I could point out that the offender's account was different. This allowed me to raise the issue I wanted to raise, but avoided problems associated with introducing another version of the crime into the court. A third example comes from a Family Court case. In an urgent report, just before a trial, I made reference to information given to me by a school principal. I was told that the classroom teacher (who had a different opinion to the principal) was giving evidence at the trial but the principal was not. Therefore, the trial judge could not consider any evidence from the principal. I therefore amended my report, as I could not draw on the material for an opinion.

There have been other instances in which I have refused to make changes to my reports. These include: a lawyer in a workers' compensation case asked me to remove a paragraph in which I outlined concern about the inconsistency of a client's information; a pre-sentence report on a dangerous offender where I was asked to remove the assessment of risk to the community; and a Family Court report where I was asked not to include test results which showed a high elevation on Antisocial Personality Disorder on one of the parties.

In my opinion, making these types of changes would have compromised my integrity as an independent professional in the opinion of the court. In all cases, I have undertaken further work for these law firms, so my principled stance does not seem to have damaged my reputation. In fact, one lawyer later complimented me for my integrity.

One of the worst examples I had to deal with involved a case in which I was asked to provide a critique of another psychologist's report. I provided this as a written report. Later, the law firm, in summarising selected extracts of my report, wanted me to swear just the sections they were interested (that is, not include the entire report). Normal practice is to swear a brief affidavit stating who I am and why I produced the report, appending the report in its entirety. The law firm did not want to include the entire report. I did not agree with the way in which they had summarised some of my opinions out of context, so I rewrote the section they had sent me. They were not happy with my response. We ended up bartering for about a week until I could get something I was ethically happy with and that the lawyer could use. This is a rare experience but unfortunately is one of the possible pitfalls.

Client Details

It is important to identify information in a legal document. Courts and lawyers work on various number systems to ensure that documents are filed correctly. Check your material for case numbers, and use those numbers. For example, a Family Court matter will have a number such as PTW 684 of 2009. This means it is a Perth Family Court case, which started in 2009. Include those numbers. These may be little things, but in many ways they are critical details.

Orientate the Reader

Writing a good report is about telling a story to the court. As with any type of story, the report has a theme, structure and purpose. I believe that all reports by professionals are written to help explain the reason for a particular situation and what the future possibilities may be. Therefore, when someone picks up the report, the first section should explain why this particular report was created. It should answer questions such as: who was the referring person, and what did they want in the report? In other words, preface the story with a brief orientation.

The initial section of the report should generally explain why you believe you are appropriately qualified for this type of assessment. I provide a few sentences summarising my experience and qualifications relevant to the particular case. I then append my curriculum vitae (CV) to the report. My CV is one page of small print (font size 10), which captures various aspects of my career especially in regards to various legal areas. I offer to provide a full ten-page résumé should further information be required. This helps the lawyer to understand whether I was suitably qualified for the type of assessment, which you will see later in this book is a critical part of the cross-examination process. By addressing the issue here (at least in brief) you will spend less time in court being qualified as a witness (unless of course you are not appropriately qualified, in which case this section will highlight your flaws and allow the court to disqualify you as a witness).

Some writers want to include in the report a full list of their experience. This then takes the first three pages. I find this quite distracting, as it focuses on the writer and not on the person being written about. It may make the author seem arrogant.

Authority

If you have followed a particular code of practice when writing a report, it is useful to make a statement to that effect. For example, in New South Wales, courts require that you make a statement that you have read the Rules for Expert Practice (for example, the District Court Rule for Expert Practice). You are then required to state that you have kept to these standards. In medico-legal areas, especially workers' compensation, there may be protocols about the type of report required. If so, state that you have written the report according to the protocols. This helps both the court and the client to understand why a report was written in a particular way.

Rule 15.62 of the Family Law Rules 2004 (Cwlth) requires an elaborate statement to be included in the affidavit attached to the report. Not only does the necessary authority need to be included, but also an awareness of the procedures, obligations and rules. As taken from the Attorney-General's Department web site, the affidavit must state:

I have made all the enquiries I believe are necessary and appropriate and to my knowledge there have not been any relevant matters omitted from this report, except as otherwise specifically stated in this report.

I believe that the facts within my knowledge that have been stated in this report are true.

The opinions I have expressed in this report are independent and impartial.

I have read and understand Part 15.5 of the Family Law Rules 2004 and have used my best endeavours to comply with it.

I have complied with the requirements of the following

professional codes of conduct or protocol, being [state the name of the code or protocol].

I understand my duty to the court and I have complied with it and will continue to do so.

In my opinion, over the next 10–20 years courts are going to insist on formal standards (and it may even get to the point of having ASO type standards for reports). Whether it gets to that level or not, there is no doubt that there are ever-increasing attempts by the courts to ensure that report writers understand their duties to the court.

Information Sources

To understand the basis of the evidence, the standard practice is to outline when and for how long the patient was seen, and by whom. An accident investigator might insert the word "accident scene" for the word "patient" and get the same outcome. This approach allows a judge to understand the standard of your work, to help them see the level of assessment used, leading them to decide how much weight to place on the case. It also allows them to put your involvement into the chronology of the case. How does it all fit together?

It is important to list accurately all of the documents you received. For reasons that will become clearer later in this book, your sources are critical for lawyers to understand the appropriateness of the evidence base. It is important to clearly list all information used in reaching your conclusions, as the credibility of your report is going to be judged against the source of your information.

With respect to information, include not only the information which is beneficial to the position you ultimately reach. The impartial expert will indicate any contrary findings and, later in the report, they will explain why such evidence exists.

Privacy Issues

Increasingly, I include in my reports a short paragraph outlining privacy issues. I state the way in which a person has consented to the release of the confidential information; that is, verbal or written consent, or on a lawyer-provided consent form. This is in case someone raises issues relating to the National Privacy Principles or places a complaint with the Registration Board. It may help me to avoid having to explain consent issues because they have been spelt out in black and white in the report.

Limitations and Cautions

In my reports I outline major limitations to the approach I took in writing the report, so that the lawyers can see if I am credible. I spell out the boundaries to the range of my report. The reader should know what I did and did not do. If something falls outside my area of expertise, then I state it, either in a separate section or in the body of the report. For example, if I have only seen the father in a Family Court dispute, I will write something like: "I have just seen the father but I understand there are two sides to every story and acknowledge I do not have the mother's version of events". The listing of major deficits allows you to go to court and not have to worry about defending yourself. It makes you look like someone who is careful and not defensive.

Do not list every weakness in your methodology as it makes you sound incompetent and opens you up for cross-examination. Listing all your weaknesses would be a tremendous boost to the opposing lawyer or barrister.

Rather, list just the obvious weaknesses that depart from normal practice to show that you have focused on the significant factors.

The court does not deem you to be an expert in everything. Only be an expert where you actually have expertise. Therefore you need to address the major limits. For example, in a Family Court matter, I was asked to do a risk assessment where there was a case of physical abuse. I was given photographs of the abuse. I needed to make a judgment, on the basis of the photos, about the severity of the abuse as one factor in offering an opinion about the degree of supervision required. However, as a psychologist, I have no special expertise in assessing bruising or injury patterns. That is exactly what I stated in my report.

Relevant History

I always include a summary of the history leading to the situation, because the dynamics are important information for setting the context of the issue. Avoid going over every detail collected unless it has relevance. For example, outlining every primary school attended, or how they performed in each grade of primary school, may only be relevant in a case where neuropsychological impairment is an issue. The nature of a building structure is relevant, but the history of that building technique may not be. In most cases the history should simply be summarised. The goal in writing the history is to tell the story so that the various items of information fit together.

Observations

One of a professional's most important pieces of information is in regards to direct observations. Under the heading of "Observations" I write comments such as: "This person's manner of speech was normal" or, "They seemed nervous because they kept fidgeting in the chair". Saying that they were dressed in blue jeans and a green T-shirt and they had a nice earring is not terribly helpful unless it is leading to something else, such as depression (that is, because of their unkempt appearance). The clinical observation is concerned with outward demeanour leading to opinions of underlying diagnosis.

For an engineer, the issues may be related to site inspections, or observations of building materials etc. Just as a clinical observation is critical for the psychologist, site observation may be critical for the engineer.

Test Results

Tests conducted by a professional are another source of information. Whether the testing is a personality test given by a psychologist, CT-scans by a radiologist, structural tests by an engineer, or a functional assessment by an occupational therapist, it is important information all of which needs to be documented. I treat test results as a separate source of information. I outline the tests I have used, including the version, and I briefly explain why I have used them.

Of critical importance, I try to explain the test results in lay terms. Unless the results are user-friendly for the non-professional, this section will be one of the least utilised areas of the report. For example, if I refer to IQ scores, most non-mental health people do not understand IQ scores. However, they do understand percentiles. I therefore write: "This person's IQ was in the average range, which means that out of 100 same-aged people they would be in the middle 50", or "This person showed fairly significant intellectual deficits, in keeping with someone who is in the bottom one in a 100 same-aged peers in the general community." It does not require training as a psychologist to follow what I am talking about. If I write a report in which complicated testing is needed, such as in a case where there has been neuropsychological testing, I will put the technical results, including raw scores, in appendices. In the body of the report I summarise the relevant tests in simple language. The appended test results keep confusing details out of the main body of the report. This allows the report to flow smoothly.

The same applies to other professions with their own standardised tests. It is critical that you make reference to the test results, but the technical aspects do not belong in the body of the report. The technical data will interfere with the flow of the report.

Terms of Reference and Discussion

When a lawyer writes to you, or a court order is made appointing you to undertake an assessment, you will usually be asked to address some questions . These are the terms of reference. It is imperative that somewhere in your report you answer the questions item by item. If you do not answer the questions, or the answers are not easy to find in the report, then you have not done a good job. The lawyer has asked these questions for good legal reasons, so try to answer them, whether or not you understand the relevance of the questions.

I once spoke to the Chief Assessor of Criminal Injuries in Western Australia about pet hates in reports. She said that it is frustrating when professionals answer questions put to them by the solicitor, but they do not list the questions they were asked. They write: "In answer to your question,

1..., 2...., 3...". The Chief Assessor would find her job much easier if the text of the questions was included.

If a lawyer approaches me for a report on a client I am seeing, I ask them to send a letter confirming this request and including the issues they would like me to address. If they do not specify the issues, it makes it difficult to know exactly what to write in the report. It is not sufficient to simply get a request for a "report". Even if you have previously written hundreds of reports, you need to know what they want in this report.

People trained in mental health approaches may be tempted to use terms like "formulation". Other mental health professionals may know what this means but most lawyers will probably not have any idea. Formulation is a great practice in the consulting room but in court you have opinions, not formulations. Avoid using a therapy approach to legal reports. If you do not formulate, what do you do? Your role is to discuss the issues.

I often find that the terms of reference do not allow me to tell the story about how a situation arose. Therefore, I have a discussion section that allows me to raise the various issues necessary to explain what is going on. In terms of a logical flow, this may come before the terms of reference, but there are no hard and fast rules as to the structure that will get the message across in the most logical and succinct fashion.

Conclusion Section

One day I was sitting in the Legal Aid Office with a lawyer when my report was delivered from the court. The lawyer flipped to the last page of my carefully constructed 18-page document in order to read my conclusion. The report was then put to one side. The moral of the story is that the last thing written in the report is often the first, and sometimes the only, section that will be read at that time (if it goes to trial you can be sure that they will read every word carefully). Careful crafting of the conclusion is paramount to your role. Of course there are pedantic lawyers who will read the report from cover to cover, so the whole thing needs to be thorough. I am not sure which style of lawyer is more concerning!

If you have written a large report, consider including an executive summary. This goes at the front of the report. It helps to orientate the reader before they put all the information together.

Appendices

Anything that interferes with the flow of the report, but may be relevant to your evidence, can be included in appendices. I include my CV, test results and other key information as appendices. These may be useful to another professional but not to the flow of the report.

Key Points

- Address your report to the court or lawyer after finding out the preferred format required by the legal system within which you are operating.

- Use appropriate reference numbers to assist with the successful processing and tracking of the report.

- All reports need to be dated, and the date must be changed if there are differing versions of a report. Before amending a report, ensure that you are not changing your opinion and that your professional obligations are being met.

- Headings are useful for arranging the data, facts, inferences and opinions into readable but discrete sections. Ensure that these different sections are kept as separate streams of information.

- Orientate the reader on the reasons for the production of the report so that they can understand your role in the process.

- Accurately document the source of all information relied upon, including information that may be detrimental to the position you hold.

- It is important to mention any cautions, limitations and obvious weaknesses of the report without making yourself look incompetent.

- The line of logical argument must be expressed in a report. The links between fact, inference and opinion must be articulated. The logic of a report should be transparent.

- Conclusions and summaries are helpful in highlighting the findings of the report. They should be written with serious consideration, as they are very important to the way in which a report is used and interpreted.

The Nuts and Bolts of Writing

This chapter started with a broad theory of writing reports, through to some of the more general aspects. The focus in this section is upon the minor nuts and bolts involved in writing a report.

First or Third Person

There is an interesting debate among practitioners about whether to use the first person singular writing style, or the third person academic style. What I typically find is that those more likely to use the third person are new graduates and those in their first five years of practice. They are still following the academic lessons they have been taught. As professionals become more experienced, they are more likely to write in the first person.

My view is that once you get past all of your indoctrination from university, first person singular is a much more powerful way of getting your opinion across, and is an effective tool for separating the fact base from the opinion. I write "my opinion" not "the report writer's opinion". Before changing your style, please make enquiries to ensure that you are meeting your professional obligations, employer's policies and procedures, and local conventions in relation to court reports.

Objective Language

Your role is to provide the court with facts. Facts are cold, hard and non-emotive. Consider the following examples that I have seen in medical reports – "The fact the psychiatrist did not prescribe the medication was a ridiculous mistake" or "This practitioner has recommended so much treatment because they are feathering their own nest". This is not objective language. The following is more objective: "The fact the psychiatrist did not prescribe medication is not consistent with the general accepted practice of treating severe depression".

Linked with objective language is the issue of ensuring that the language is jargon free. We need to ensure that the meaning of explicit terms and abbreviations are clearly documented. Within a profession, new terms emerge. Just out of interest, try getting three people of the age of 45 years old to tell you the exact meaning of SMS, MSN, and ATM. These are everyday terms for younger people. Where terms simply change (for example, intellectual disability was previously called mental retardation), it is important to ensure that judges have a bridge between old and new terms. Try putting the old term in brackets after the new term so that judges can learn as terminology changes. There may be as much as a five-year time lag between the terminology professionals use compared to that understood by those outside the profession.

Another type of emotive language to avoid is argumentative language. You are not there to argue with people, you are a scientist. Avoid commenting on the credibility of others. If you see reports from other people, do not say, for example: "They do not know what they are talking about, they are only a new graduate". I tend to say very little about other people when I write my reports. It is my opinion and others are allowed to have their opinion.

Using Pronouns

Words like "he", "she" and "it" are necessary to avoid writing full names every time. However, these little words can be misleading if they are not clearly defined in the writing process. There may be more than one "he" in a report. I am not saying that you should not use pronouns, but you have to be very clear to whom you are referring, and if you cannot make it clear, people could get confused.

Sometimes I see terms like: "We assessed the structure and found ..." I would ask how many people assessed this structure. If it was two or three, then after having listed who conducted the visit, then the use of "we" is appropriate. If it was just one person, the royal "we" is being used. The use of the royal "we" sounds very arrogant.

Less formal than pronouns are vague expressions like: "it is said" (for example, it is said that the playground equipment was ten years old). You need to be more precise. Relying on vague supposition puts you in a more risky position. The more precise you can be, the better your evidence will survive cross-examination.

Using Words Carefully

Scientific certainty is really interesting when discussed with lawyers, as they view probability differently to us. Until about three years ago, I frequently used the term "probability" in my reports because, as someone trained in statistics, probability equals high certainty. Scientists learn probability rates, and if we say it was probable, or highly probable, we mean it is quite likely. Lawyers actually use the word "probability" in the opposite sense. They think probability means doubt. From the legal perspective, if it is probable, you do not really know. For example: "It was probable that Mrs Paulson's injury was caused by the accident". As a health worker, you say: "Well that means that the injury was caused by the accident". Lawyers consider that there is doubt around the issue of whether the injury was caused by the accident.

There are various other terms of a similar nature, which need care when including them in a report. "Presumably", "evidently", "there appears to be" – these all imply hearsay. You need to avoid the implication that you don't really know something. "It seems", "could", "apparently", "I believe" – are all similar in their connotations. "I have assessed someone for an opinion", "I do not believe it is likely", "in my opinion it is likely".

Words like "complete", "thorough", "meticulous", and "exhaustive" – are words you may also wish to avoid. "I did an exhaustive view of the documents". The lawyer will pull out a little document and ask whether you have seen it, and you have to say no. How exhaustive was your review? "I did a meticulous assessment of this person". The lawyer might ask: "Well what other assessments do you do" – "quick and nasty?". There are implications if you go too far one way or the other. You have to watch your language and keep it balanced.

Avoid personal, political, or moral statements in a report. Moralise to government departments, or to professional bodies, but not in the actual court report. Soapboxes have no place in court. If there is a shortage of a particular service, state it as a fact relevant to the report, not as a political issue. For example, there may be insufficient services for counselling children in a country town, but do not state: "Due to the government's failure to act, there are insufficient services ...". Instead state: "When considering the costing for future services, in this case a travel allowance will also need to be considered as the nearest city which provides this type of service is ...". The first is a soapbox response; the second is an objective fact relevant to the case.

Tenses

If something has been collected in the past, I will refer to it in the past tense. Most assessment is in the past. However, the current tense makes an opinion more alive. Therefore current tense opinions can be helpful. However, bear in mind that a report is probably only going to be read a year or more after it was written, and you collected the information days, weeks or months beforehand, so a lot of the information will be presented in the past tense. There is no simple view on it, but try to be consistent with your use of tenses.

Key Points

- The first person is useful in reports as it makes it clear what is your opinion and what is the evidence base. Ensure that this writing style is consistent with local conventions and employer policies.

- Language should be non-emotive, precise and clear. Define terms and avoid jargon. Choose your words carefully.

- Pronouns should be used carefully in order to avoid ambiguity in relation to the person the report is referring to.

4

The Reliable Witness

As you approach the time to give evidence in court, hopefully you have handled the lawyer's initial request well and have positioned yourself to be as independent as the circumstances allowed. You should have provided a carefully crafted report to either the briefing lawyer or the court. The next step is to give evidence in court. You are now in a position to become a reliable or credible witness.

The Reliable Witness

Understanding the Role

The concept of a reliable witness is interesting. As a psychologist, I have been taught that validity concerned whether a test measured what it was supposed to measure (that is, did it give a true measure), and reliability concerned getting the same results each time a test was administered.

However, in law, the terms are used in almost the opposite way. A reliable witness is not someone who turns up on time or gives the same answer each time – a reliable witness is someone who is seen by the court to be truthful. A reliable witness provides information that can be relied upon.

To understand the concept of a reliable witness it is important to understand evidence from a lawyer's point of view. To explain this I will begin with a philosophical question: what is truth? The following example, provided by a Western Australian forensic pathologist, illustrates the issue. A fatal train accident occurred at an outer suburban rail crossing. A number of witnesses on a railway platform heard a bang, and saw a boom gate come down onto the bonnet of a car as the car travelled across the railway crossing. The car was smashed by a passenger train. All of the witnesses said that they saw the boom gate come down onto the car. In other words, their evidence pointed to a mechanical fault in the boom gate. This particular suburb has a problem with crime, so a number of security cameras were operating on the platform. One of these security cameras captured what happened at the railway crossing. The video showed that the car hit the boom gate (causing the bang that the witnesses had heard) and forced the boom gate up rapidly. The witnesses had turned and seen the boom gate coming down for a second time, followed by the train hitting the car. The truth was that the accident was not caused by a mechanical failure in the boom gate, but human error on the part of the driver. The issue highlighted in this example is that the direct truth may not be known. The court was not present, and rarely does the court have a video of what happened. The court uses witnesses to infer a version of the truth based on evidence.

As professionals, there is no objective reality to much of our work, only theoretical constructs. Symptoms and signs are observed and diagnoses are inferred. The lack of direct observation is why different professionals often make different judgments. Take, for example, an air-conditioning engineer. The engineer will use smoke streams at the outlet of the vents to see how the air is being distributed, and then adjust the various baffles in the system. He cannot see the air, but he can see the smoke. From this he can postulate the airflows and infer whether the problems are due to the baffles, the air filters or the fans.

The court tries to make a finding based on the witnesses' reports. The court makes findings to help infer the "truth". There are different methods of doing this but the one commonly used in Australian courts is the adversarial system. For example, if I said I had a piece of string, how do you actually know it is a piece of string unless you see it? The way society makes such determinations is to appoint an independent person (a judge) to oversee the situation, and then have two sides test the case. If I had one person look at the string, they might say: "That is a nice piece of string, it has got fibres twisted together, it is the colour of string, the size of string, so it must be string". If I then gave the string to somebody else for a critical assessment, they might say: "No, that is not a piece of string." That person pulls it and tries to break it, and then argues about the makeup of the fibres. Finally, the judge decides whether or not it is a piece of string based on what he or she has been told, but without ever seeing it.

In the real world, it does not matter whether or not it is string as long as it ties things together. The truth does matter in court so the evidence must be tested. In court someone will initially go over your report to draw out the strengths. Then someone else will pick holes in your report to prove that it is not a good report. Finally, a judge rules on how well the report measured up. Lawyers call this process testing the evidence. Untested evidence cannot be relied upon, however, tested evidence is very useful to lawyers and judges.

When first provided to the court your report is untested. However, as the author, you believe the report to be the truth. This is why so many professionals find court such a taxing process. We "know" what we wrote is true and we believe that we have done our work to the best of our abilities. We then go to court where some lawyer tries to say that we got some or all of it wrong. If you can understand that the court does not have first-hand access to the truth, only to witnesses who bring material to the court, the perspective changes. It is not about you as a person. It is a process whereby people who were not there when the event happened test the evidence. Once the evidence has undergone the rigours of the testing process the court can put weight on it. However, if you have not done a good job in setting up the situation, when they tug the string, the report falls apart. The manner of testing is discussed later.

The Threat to Good Evidence

In an interesting article by Dvoskin and Guy (2008, p.203) the authors point out that most errors are related to our egos. They state:

It is our position that the most egregious errors by expert witnesses are almost always attributable to narcissistic needs, including the need to praised, the need to make money, the need to be right, and to win.

The authors explain that being a star witness at a trial has a seductive appeal and professionals enjoy the feelings associated with being important. This leads them to care excessively about image and, in the process, lose what the expert should focus on; that is, the truth. They describe yielding to these needs as "a dangerous and slippery slope". The expert who wants to win will be tempted to embellish their evidence to make it more appealing. Those who need to be admired will be tempted to enhance their qualifications, expertise and other experiences to appear better than they really are. If someone is money orientated, they may say what the lawyers want to hear in order to make their opinion more marketable.

The authors' solution is the same as that emphasised in this book; that is, an expert is merely another source of evidence. Evidence that is truthful, unembellished, and with flaws admitted, is of most help to the court. I would add that the best experts are also "scientific computers" - they can analyse different information and provide opinions related to different fact bases.

Communication with Lawyers

I have had considerable contact with lawyers, which includes running training for lawyers. As a result, I have become interested in lawyers' thought processes. I have observed that lawyers communicate in terms of evidence and fact. Lawyers love their facts and they want logic. Hard scientists find this compatible with their own mindset but many professionals, such as mental health professionals, social workers, and counsellors are less concerned about objective reality; they are interested in motive, emotion and dynamics. Therefore there are two very distinct views or, in other terms, different narratives. The medical doctor is more likely to be interested in fact (for example, whether a disease is present or absent), but the language used to communicate this fact will be a very different narrative than that used by the lawyer.

I remember the moment when this insight hit home; it was in the middle of a trial in relation to a young man who had been diagnosed by a psychiatrist as suffering from bi-polar disorder. In his manic state he had stolen a car, and was attempting to drive to Sydney to fly to New York to take over the jaguar car factory because his name was similar. The factory was not in America, let alone New York. He could not tell me why he had to drive to Sydney to fly to America. But the prosecutor said to me: "The fact of the matter is it not, is that he is a 17-year-old in a stolen car, caught out of Kalgoorlie?" I replied with an obvious "yes" to which the prosecutor replied: "And how does that prove he has got bi-polar disorder?" The fact of the matter was that he was driving a stolen car. What I was interested in was the intent. Fortunately, the judge was also interested in intent and, at the end of the day, I helped the judge understand that it was more likely than not that it was the bi-polar disorder that had motivated the young man's actions.

These patterns of communication are similar to male to female communication documented in the popular literature (such as in John Gray's "Men are from Mars, Women are from Venus"). Lawyers take the more factually based "male" style, while the mental health professional tends to use the emotive "female" style. What we are dealing with are two systems of communication. In psychotherapy, there has been an increasing interest in Narrative Therapy and how the dominant narrative wins the communication conflict. Unfortunately, what happens is that when we talk to lawyers in court they are the dominant narrative. If we use our skills, we can understand that all we are doing is communicating with someone who communicates in a different way. The path to better understanding becomes clear. Logic, fact and reason are the language of legal process and we must work in that narrative.

My first lawyer friend was a lady by the name of Kate Stockwell. I used to ring her up at work sometimes, and she would be in "lawyer-mode". Her abrupt manner seemed cold and harsh. The phone call was simply: "yes, yes, and no", click! Afterwards I would think: "what have I done to upset her?" It was as if the friendly, chatty woman I knew had been possessed by an alien. With time, I stopped personalising her reactions and came to realise that all she was doing was dealing with facts in the business-like manner of a lawyer. If you speak to a lawyer and waffle on about emotional stuff, you should understand that you will lose them. Think through the facts and present them first. If you think they need the warm fuzzy stuff, give it to them at the end.

Another issue in relation to communication is highlighted in the following example in which I was involved in a Care and Protection Hearing in the Children's Court in Western Australia. I had to wait for another psychologist to give evidence. As I had been appointed as expert in the Children's Court, I was allowed to sit at the back of the court and watch the other psychologist give evidence (normally witnesses have to wait outside). The psychologist had carried out some psychometric testing and was discussing the fact that the elevations were indicative of somatic complaints. The lawyer said to her: "What does this test profile mean when the client was stressed?" The psychologist replied: "It would most likely result in somatic complaints". The lawyer said: "You mean complaints against the welfare department?" She was really nervous and said: "Yes, and the client will have physical illnesses". In that little interaction, the court and the two lawyers were left thinking that somatic complaints originated from some sort of sick litigious person who was going to sue government departments when stressed. The witness seemed like quite a sensible practitioner but because she was nervous and she used a jargon that the court did not understand, the court was misled. Fortunately, I gave evidence after her and was able to correct the misunderstanding and explain that psychosomatic complaints are physical symptoms caused by psychological processes. Whatever jargon you use, whether medical, psychological, from the sciences, or accounting, take care to ensure that correct meanings are conveyed.

If you are ever in the position where you realise that you are unintentionally misleading the court, it is appropriate for you to say: "I think my answers have been misleading the court". This is a line that gets them to stop in their tracks, as the court does not want to be misled. If you then say: "Look, sorry but I feel that I am creating a misunderstanding, can I clarify that answer?" Usually the lawyer who asked you the question will say: "no" as they are happy to have your answer go down a wrong path, but the other lawyer usually jumps up and says: "yes, we need to hear what he or she has got to say". As judges need to be informed, they may seek to have the situation clarified. Even if you do not get to clarify your position, the judge will know that you made a mistake and will consider that when they weigh up the evidence.

Rules of Evidence

Rules of evidence are principles of law that determine what may or may not be admitted as evidence in court. There are whole law books on rules of evidence, as it is a complex area of law. As such, a detailed understanding requires legal advice. However, I will provide my perspective to help explain certain aspects of these rules and to highlight areas where you may need to seek legal advice.

Take, for example, the following hypothetical situation. A man called Rod comes into a seminar room in which I am conducting a workshop, trips over the power cord to my projector and damages his hip in the fall. After running up $10,000 of medical expenses, missing months of work, and being told he will never play professional football again, he sues me, and the hotel, for negligence. Everyone at the workshop who saw what happened is now a potential witness. In court these types of people are the best witnesses as they saw what happened. This is evidence from the direct observers – they are witnesses of fact. A fact in a legal sense is something that is directly perceived through one of the five senses.

Normally, in court, the only person allowed to give evidence is someone who is a witness of fact. In giving evidence, such witnesses are not allowed to offer a reason why Rod fell. To say that the power cord was wrongly placed or that Rod was clumsy are opinions. Opinion evidence can only be given by people deemed to have expertise over and beyond normal people. This select group of people are the experts.

Suppose you were at my workshop and went home after seeing the fall. You excitedly say to your spouse: "Wow, something amazing happened today. This participant Rod came running in, tripped over a power cord, hurt himself, left in an ambulance and now he is suing everybody. I may have to go to court as a witness of fact". If your partner was called to court, he or she did not see the fall themselves. They only know what you told them. Their evidence would be called hearsay. There are some very significant implications for hearsay evidence. For example, if you spoke to a mother while assessing a child, and the mother did not give evidence, anything told to you by the mother could be disallowed as hearsay.

Steffen v Ruban (1966) is a precedent that is still followed. It is a New South Wales case that illustrates the principle of admissibility of evidence. In the case a medical doctor expressed opinions partly derived from what he had been told by the mother of a child, and partly from the child (the child is the complainant). The mother was called as a witness but was too emotionally affected to give any more than brief evidence of the child's condition. The child was not called as a witness to the court. (As an aside, under rules of evidence, a professional can give evidence on behalf of a child. This evidence is not hearsay, even if the child never goes to court.

The same evidence from a parent would be classed as hearsay.) The court in this case noted:

It cannot be clear from Dr Bailey's evidence whether he was expressing conclusions based on his own observations or based on what he had been told by the boy's mother. If his conclusions were mainly based on what he had been told by the boy's mother then there is no evidence from her that what she had told the doctor was correct, and in the present case this is of vital importance. If any part of Dr Bailey's evidence was sufficiently clear, based on his own observations or tests, one could say that, despite deficiencies in the proof of the history of the child, the medical evidence was clear nevertheless, and there is no reason to interfere with the verdict. However, I find it quite impossible to say this on Dr Bailey's evidence ((Steffen v Ruban [1966]2 NSWR 622).

In this case Dr Bailey was not clear about the information he got from the mother and the information he got from the child. His Honour concluded:

If his evidence is such that it's impossible to analyse what the conclusions are based on his own observations and what the conclusions are based on what he had been told, then in such a case as the present one, the danger of mistrial becomes very great (p. 624).

The implications from this judgment are twofold. The first is that if someone tells you something, and that person is not going to court as a witness, that piece of information may not be admissible evidence. If it is not admissible in evidence, you cannot use it to offer an opinion in your assessment. The second is that you must make it very clear in your report what you directly hear, observe or test, and what comes from somewhere else, including documents and third party witnesses. If Dr Bailey had made it clear which parts of the information had been from the mother and from the child, then the judge may have been able to make a decision.

Unfortunately, the judge could not tell so he had no choice but to order another trial.

I have experienced two situations in the Family Court in which what seemed like good evidence dissolved to hearsay. In one example, I had spoken to, and received information from, a child's principal at school. The classroom teacher, and not the principal, was called to give evidence at the trial. The teacher's evidence was almost opposite to what I had been told by the principal. I had to disregard everything I had been told by the principal and change my opinions in light of the teacher's evidence. This was no easy task in the middle of a cross-examination. In the second example, I had interviewed a 19-year-old who allegedly had been sexually abused by her uncle when she was a 13-year-old. I had spoken to the uncle. At the trial the uncle was not called as a witness. The young lady became too upset to give evidence and the court decided not to hear from her. Despite having a partial confession and detailed witness statement I was instructed to disregard that evidence, as the court had not heard from either witness. It can be heartbreaking to know what I believed to be the truth, but be unable to express it because of these rules of evidence. From my perspective it seems very unfair. However, in terms of legal process, for a judge to make a decision without proper evidence, the process would be legally unfair.

At the risk of being repetitive, when you write your report you should draw clear distinctions between an observation, your reasoning, and your opinions. I use lots of terms like "it is my opinion", and "it is my understanding". I avoid the term "I believe" as it is not an act of faith. Nor do I use terms like "best guess" as guessing will not assist a court. Judge Wisbey commented on this issue as follows:

In order to facilitate a proper appreciation of the opinion, and a sound evaluation of that opinion and its validity, it is essential that facts upon which the opinion is based are clearly identified. This then enables the application of commonsense and logic to be used to determine the validity of the opinion. The application of forensic logic should generally provide the answer. It is important to indicate clearly in any report or in evidence, that part of the report or evidence that is based on ascertained fact, and which is inferential (i.e. conclusions drawn from objective fact).

Key Points

- A reliable witness is the witness who produces evidence that the court can rely upon.

- There is very little objective truth for the court to see first hand, as the judge or jury were not there at the time. The court has to rely on the evidence of witnesses who provide information (facts) so that the court can make a determination.

- Evidence is tested by cross-examination to determine whether or not something is true.

- Most avoidable errors made by expert witnesses are almost always attributable to narcissistic needs, including the need to praised, the need to make money, the need to be right, and the need to win.

- Witnesses who understand that they are simply a piece of evidence give the best testimony.

- Lawyers consider information in terms of logic and fact. Therefore those from factual professions, such as engineering and medicine, have an easier time than those from professions that focus on motivations and intents, such as psychologists and counsellors.

- Rules of evidence determine what information will be allowed in court. These rules are complex and differ in relation to evidence from children and adults. The rules are specific to the court in which they are practiced.

- Make clear the distinction between what you directly observe (facts) and your opinions. Ensure that the reader can follow your line of reasoning.

Expert Evidence

The Expert

In his paper Judge Wisbey states: "... opinion evidence (that is the opinion of a witness as to the facts) is generally inadmissible." As mentioned earlier, most witnesses cannot have an opinion, they can only report on the fact of what they have perceived through their senses. Judge Wisbey continues:

It is for the trial judge to draw all the necessary inferences or conclusions from the evidence presented. ... Opinions by experts are an exception to the general rule to which I have referred. Expert evidence is admissible whenever the subject matter of the enquiry is such that inexperienced persons are unlikely to prove capable of forming a correct judgment upon it without such assistance, in other words, when it so far partakes of the nature of a science as to require a course of previous habit, or study, in order to the attainment of a knowledge of it.

It is very important when giving evidence that you do not overstep your area of expertise. The minute you start offering opinions on things that are based on lay understanding, you have ceased to be an expert offering an opinion. However, you may be called to offer opinions on medications when you are not medically trained, offer opinions on bruise patterns when you do not have a degree in injury patterns, to or discuss theories of electrical engineering when you are mechanically trained. If possible, recognise when you are being asked to cross the line.

You do not have to be an expert in everything, just those things which are relevant to your assessment or evaluation.

Judge Wisbey notes that there are three conditions that must be fulfilled before evidence can be received as expert evidence. The first is:

A witness cannot qualify as an expert unless his or her profession, habit or a course of study or experience gives him or her a greater capacity of judging the issue than is possessed by other people.

The person giving the evidence must demonstrate that he or she has the necessary qualifications to speak about the subject matter.

On one occasion I was asked to give evidence in a rape trial in relation to a person who had suffered a brain injury as a child and who was a heavy marijuana smoker. I was going to give evidence on the effects of marijuana smoking on brain injury and some of the consequent implications. It was decided that expert psychological evidence was not necessary because the ordinary people of the jury were capable of judging that issue. The court was of the opinion that the normal person in the street knows enough about brain injury and marijuana use to make good judgments.

While talking about habit, I found the following anecdote a really fascinating example of the ability to provide expert evidence: "A heroin addict has been held, by reason of experience in dealing with what is purported to be heroin, to be sufficiently equipped to offer an opinion as to whether a particular substance was heroin" (Price v R [1981] TasR 306 CCA). So a heroin addict is an expert on heroin because of their previous habit. They are only going to be able to give a very limited range of opinion evidence.

The second condition noted by Judge Wisbey is:

The qualifications or expertise must relate to a matter which is capable of being the subject of expertise – that is of training and/or experience placing the person possessing it in a position to form an educated opinion on the matter not capable of being formed by persons generally.

This is self-explanatory.

The third condition according Judge Wisbey is:

No expert is entitled to deal with a question, the answer to which ultimately depends upon the application of a legal standard ...

This condition refers to the ultimate issue, which was discussed in the previous chapter.

If you gain only one thing from this book, it is this point: "Courts look to experts for well-grounded opinions based on scientific neutrality, rather than disguised personal preferences or speculation" (McCann & Dyer, 1996, p.34). If your position is scientifically neutral, you will be a good expert. The more you align to an outcome, a position, or a person, the less favourably the court will perceive your evidence. I once read something to the effect of: "the perfect expert is someone who has no investment in any particular outcome".

A Western Australian state forensic pathologist, at a forensic college meeting about DNA testing, provided a great example, which illustrates the principle of neutrality. She said that she did not know to whom the samples belonged, and she did not care. She said that she did not care to whom the samples were being compared. All she cared about was the probability that two samples were either the same or different and the variables that might affect the probability. If you can achieve a position of being a computer of variables related to your area of expertise, then you will do well in court. If you want to become rigid, and dig in your heels, then you will do very badly.

Judge Wisbey describes that key point in this way: "It is essential that the expert remain impartial to the cause, and appreciate that his or her obligation is to the truth (the court) rather than the party who has engaged them". When you are in court, you work for the court not a client. Your role is to provide the judge with the truth so that they can make a decision. This may raise some ethical issues because, in many professions, the ethical standard states explicitly that the practitioner has an overriding obligation to the client. However, knowing the court's expectations allows you to structure your presentation to accommodate the competing needs. Most inexperienced professionals do not understand their obligation to the court as expert witnesses, and therefore create frustration and confusion for both themselves and the court.

As noted by Judge Wisbey, according to an article in the University of Chicago Law Review, American expert witnesses have become known as "saxophones", because the attorneys play the tune, manipulating the expert to make the sounds they want! You do not want to be known as a saxophone, as that would be the opposite of what it takes to be a good expert. You do not want to be manipulated. Lawyers do play games and they try to get evidence to support their position. However, I have a reputation for impartiality and I hang on to that reputation with as much vigour as I can. If I am asked to provide a second opinion report, and I say something that is contrary to what the lawyers hoped for, I still say it. I may try to write it in a way that is beneficial to their position in court, but I try not to get sucked into writing something for the sake of getting future referrals.

There are professionals who are happy to work for just one party to a dispute. These are the so-called "hired guns". In every profession there are people who have set positions. When you hear that they have produced a report, even without reading it you already know what their findings will be. In my opinion, this position is reprehensible. All cases are different, and each case should be examined on its own merits, leading to its own outcome. The one-sided position generates income but, in my opinion, those practitioners have sold out their professional integrity and are causing damage to the wider profession's reputation. Where possible, I try to do some work for both sides of the situation. I like to work for defence and prosecution, insurer and claimant, or offender and victim. It helps to stay balanced. Unfortunately, it is not always possible. For example, in Western Australia, prosecution reports are generally produced in-house, while the defence uses outsourced experts.

Impartiality has implications for attending court. Statistically, less than two in ten of my independent and comprehensive Family Court reports end up in a trial. In reality this means I rarely go to court even when I am dealing with serious allegations occurring in complex situations. If I give party evidence by working for just one side or the other, I estimate that approximately five in ten reports go to trial. Therefore, the better your report, and the more objective you are perceived to have been, the less frequently the report will be challenged.

Perhaps the most important aspect to consider is with whom in the courtroom does the role of advocacy belong? A lawyer is the advocate for the client in the courtroom, not you. You are an advocate for the profession and an advocate for the truth, but not for the client.

Considering the Judge's Perspective

It does not take long for most professionals to work out what fact, opinion and hearsay are, and they take care not to include it in their reports. This is good practice. However, the acceptance of my reports in court shifted markedly for the better when the penny finally dropped and I realised that it was not my perspective of the evidence, but the judge's perspective, which counts.

For example, I wrote a report in which I had spoken to a mother, a child, but not the grandmother (not enough funding to talk to everyone). From my perspective, what the child and mother told me is fact. Any information I have in relation to the grandmother is hearsay, because the mother told it to me. The mother subsequently "did a runner" to a secret overseas destination, taking the child with her. She did not file any affidavits. However, her mother went to court to give evidence. My interview with the child was considered by the judge to be fact, because children cannot themselves give evidence. Anything the mother told me was now hearsay, because the judge could not test it, and the information from the grandmother would be considered by the judge to be fact. Can you see how the perspective shifted? My report would only be as good as the facts given to the court.

It is impossible to know exactly who will attend court and which facts the judge will have access to. However, if you consider the judge's perspective of what is likely to be seen as fact, you will write reports which are markedly more defensible and less open to cross-examination.

As a result of talking to a peripheral witness (that is, one who would not normally be called), who you have determined to be of special relevance for your evidence, you may want to suggest that the court hears from that person. For example: "Having considered the views of Mr Smith, I am of the opinion that it is important he is called as a witness so the judge can determine whether he considers the evidence in the same light." Whether the lawyers actually call that person or not is outside of your control, but at least you have flagged the option.

Do not write about the judge's perspective in your report. If you are seen to be telling the judge what they think, you will find yourself in hot water. In one report, I said something to the effect of: "A judge is likely to find ...". The judge told me in no uncertain terms that he did not like to be told what he would find. At best, I was seen to be arrogant. At worst, I could be seen to be contemptuous.

Parallel Streams of Information

Once you have mastered the importance of fact and opinion from a judge's perspective, it is critical to understand how to structure that information so that it is defensible. The strategy relates to the way in which information should be structured for both writing the report and surviving court.

Parallel streaming of fact works like this. You have your opinion. Your opinion is based on your test data, observations and provided facts. That is, three separate streams of information. It is possible to break it into more streams. For example, direct observations and professional skill. An engineer can look at the gauges of a machine as well as observe the sounds of the motor. A psychologist can have reported history and clinical observation.

What this means is that if you have this information clearly sorted in your report and you are questioned, for example: "Dr Watts, you used the Rorschach (a test of questionable reliability) in this assessment. You've got to concede that the Rorschach has some degree of questionable reliability". I would then use my usual Rorschach defensive strategy and, if that did not work, I could either panic or realise that I have other means of justifying my opinions. If the lawyer knocks out the projective testing, I still have other legs to stand on. This is because my information is in clear parallel streams and each stream has been used to build up the picture.

If you jumble all your information together in a general section (rather than in sections with headings), which is the tendency of someone when they first start to write reports, you would go into panic mode as your evidence is knocked out. If you do not realise that you have the other streams of data, one knocked out source could send you off the edge. If you have got the streams of information clearly set out in your report (and in your mind), it is not a fatal blow, but a minor injury. Several more sections would have to be knocked out before you are left with nothing to rely upon. That is how I conceptualise my information section.

Acting as a Reliable Witness

In bringing together the threads of the discussion so far, the expert functioning as a reliable witness will operate on a number of dimensions. These include:

Neutral Versus Partisan

Are you seen as a seeker of the truth or are you just confirming a position? Lawyers get to know your position very quickly and if you have a pattern of findings you will be labelled accordingly. Obviously the truth seeker will be seen in a much better light.

Judge Wisbey, when speaking about the tendency for witnesses to become partisan, states:

... it is important not to lose sight of the fact that a conflict in expert view, reflecting genuine differences of opinion based upon the then state of the psychological science, and perhaps reflecting the patient's presentation, is an important part of the adversarial system.

Judges accept that we do not have to agree with one another. Just because someone has a different view, it does not mean it is wrong.

With respect to neutrality, also note that trying too hard to win a case will make you seem just as partisan as if you'd tried to discredit another practitioner's position. The term "neutral", meaning neither for nor against (or the middle ground), makes perfect sense.

Objective Versus Subjective

Are you offering a reasoned opinion based on the evidence or based on personal preferences and opinions? If you are objective you will do well in court, but if you are subjective you deserve to get shot down in court.

Subjectivity becomes evident when emotion slips into the writing of a report. The more emotive the material, the more the position has gone from scientific neutrality into subjective speculation. You are offering lay opinion not scientific opinion.

Flexible Versus Rigid

Does your opinion change with hypothetical scenarios and other information? When I first started to attend court as a witness, I used to dig my heels in when hypothetical propositions were made. I would say: "Oh, no, that did not happen", that is, I would argue whether or not the hypothetical had occurred. I subsequently learned that I would be seen in a better light if I prefaced the answer but addressed their question. For example: "I found no evidence of that, but if it happened this would be my opinion." You have now become a computer able to adjust expert variables. This is critically important. If you came into the trial on day three, you would not know what had happened during the first two days. You may be asked to consider something as a hypothetical situation, which later turns out to be real.

Judge Wisbey describes this point as follows:

There are often occasions when an expert, confronted during his or her evidence with material of which he or she was not previously aware, will not be prepared to acknowledge that it has any relevance or impact on his or her opinion. It is important that you are prepared to accommodate new material and to acknowledge that it impacts upon your opinion if that is the case. A witness should not be frightened to indicate to the trial judge that he or she would need time to reflect on the new material before indicating whether or not it affects the opinion that has been expressed.

This importance of flexibility of position will be examined further when cross-examination is discussed in the next chapter.

Co-operative Versus Defensive

I heard about a colleague, whom I did not know very well, who had argued with a judge and had challenged the subpoena to produce his counselling notes. The practitioner argued: "I don't want to show you my notes", to which the judge replied: "Well you have to". The practitioner then said: "But the notes are confidential". The judge, seemingly unimpressed with this argument, said: "I have ordered you to show me your notes, if you do not I can gaol you for contempt of court". The practitioner foolishly replied: "But no, they're confidential"! This was an unwise stance, as it would not have helped his evidence one iota. He had lost any credibility he may have had, due to his lack of understanding of the law. If he had understood that he was there to assist the court, he could have expressed his concerns in relation to confidentiality, and then handed over the notes having fulfilled any ethical obligation he felt about releasing confidential information.

Image in court is a critical variable, which is in your hands. If you are seen to be willing to help the court you will in no way jeopardise your evidence. In fact, the opposite is likely to be the case. The co-operative witness gains credibility with the court.

Sale of Time Versus Sale of Opinion

A hired gun is someone who has opinions for sale. Everyone knows what they will write and the market seeks those opinions. This may result in short-term gains for an individual but can damage the credibility of the entire profession. A reliable witness is someone who sells time. They conduct a thorough assessment and provide reasonable opinions. The opinion remains the same, no matter which side has paid for it.

It is important to realise that you do not have to apologise for being paid for the work you do. You are entitled to reasonable remuneration for the services you've rendered. Lawyers know that better than anybody, as they are well-known for their billing practices. Most professional witnesses are paid a lot less than the lawyers cross-examining them, even though they may have undertaken many more years of study.

Key Points

- Opinion evidence is governed by special rules. Your qualifications and experience will determine whether you meet the necessary standard to be a witness, but it is the issue at hand which the court will use to determine whether they need the assistance of an expert.

- It is essential for a witness to stay within their area of expertise. Just because you are in the witness box, it does not mean that you will be able to answer all the questions.

- Courts look to experts for well-grounded opinions based on scientific neutrality, rather than disguised personal preferences or speculation.

- It is essential that the expert remains impartial to the cause, and appreciates that his or her obligation is to the truth (the court) rather than to the party who has engaged them

- The court and your profession do not need witnesses who provide opinions to suit an issue or position. These "hired guns" do all of us a disservice.

- You are an advocate for the truth, not the client.

- Considering information from the judge's perspective helps to identify hearsay. If the judge can't test it, it should not be in the report.

- Parallel streams of information help ensure survival in the witness box. It allows a structure to separate fact sources into defensible sections of information that stand alone.

- The neutral, objective witness, whose purpose is to assist the court, will find that their impartiality, and the weight the court puts on their material, enhanced.

- The partisan, rigid or hostile witness will end up being poorly received by the court. At best, their evidence may not be given much weight and, at worst, they will be seen to waste the court's time.

5

In the Witness Box

Introduction

In this chapter I will share some of the practical aspects of going to court. In the first section, I will discuss how evidence is tested, describe what lawyers or barristers try to do with their examination of witnesses, and then discuss some strategies to help you to survive the experience. However, prior to the discussion of these points, a few comments about the research on credibility may be helpful.

Credibility

Dvoskin and Guy (2008, pp.205-206) note that careful attention to credibility is important because once credibility is impeached it is very difficult to recover. In social psychology, three sets of variables underpin credibility:

expertise, trustworthiness, and dynamism. Expertise is addressed elsewhere in this book (but some aspects warrant further discussion), while the two remaining areas deserve some specific comment.

Research exists which suggests that jurors prefer mental health testimony from experts who are more clinically orientated and have practical experience rather than from those who are purely academic. I would expect this finding applies across other professions and to all triers of fact. Therefore, it is important that assessors ensure that they maintain at least some practical application for their work.

Research has also been undertaken in relation to the speaking style of witnesses. Witnesses who had a powerful speaking style and spoke with confidence were well received. This included: speaking with assertiveness; avoiding the use of intensifiers, hedges, and excessively polite forms of language; expressing confidence in oneself when asked to do so; providing descriptive answers to lawyers' questions; and avoiding hyper-correct speech (that is, not being overly formal).

Nonverbal communications can help to present a powerful image to the court. Dvoskin and Guy cite research to indicate that the clarity of the expert's speech, familiarity with the facts of the case, and impartiality were relatively more important in establishing credibility compared to academic credentials, personality or appearance. The latter were substantial.

The Process of Testing the Evidence

Swearing In

When you walk into court, you must first be sworn in. You either swear an oath (on the Bible) or make an affirmation (to tell the truth). I believe that it is also possible to swear on other holy books as long as they are recognised by the court.

In days gone past, our word used to mean something. These days, when someone gives you their word, it probably lasts as long as it takes to say it. The swearing in is a custom that is considered by the court to be important. It is supposed to mean something and historically (that is, during the last century) people would use expressions like "my word is my bond", and meant it. Hopefully, you do tell the truth because you believe in that process.

At a legal level a sworn document or sworn witness has a special place in the court system. The person or documents become locked into the legal matter. To fail to tell the truth will no longer be a case of simply lying, but of perverting the course of justice, or perjury.

Evidence-in-Chief

The first part of the testing of your evidence is the evidence-in-chief. The lawyer who has called you to give evidence is generally the person who will lead you through your evidence. There are several formalities that usually take place. First, you will be asked to state your name, address and qualification. The lawyer goes through the processes of qualifying you as a witness by highlighting the expertise you have and its relevance to the case. This varies from simply stating your qualification to a detailed examination of your skills and expertise.

Generally, you have written a report and a copy of the report is formally tendered to the judge by the lawyer. This process involves you seeing a copy and stating that it is the report you wrote. If there is more than one version of your report, do make sure that the correct one was tendered. At the point of tendering your report, any errors of significance should be raised. It is better to have everyone include the word "not" in the sentence now rather than once your evidence is under way!

During the next part of the evidence-in–chief, the lawyer will draw out from you the information relevant to their position. Generally, the lawyer will say nice things about your report (unless your report was unfavourable and they had to tender it anyway, in which case they may be quite biting in their examination).

Please remember that although they may be your briefing lawyer, they are not your lawyer. You are a witness, not a client, and they do not have any obligation to you. Their role is to use you for evidence and to advocate for their client. They are not to be relied upon to help you. They will only assist you in so far as it is a benefit to their client.

Cross-examination

After the "friendly" lawyer has finished, the opposition's job is to represent their client's position, in particular, by exposing the flaws and the weaknesses in your report. The cross-examination is the part of giving evidence that every witness dreads. This is the confrontational aspect of the adversarial approach. The cross-examining lawyer's job is to show that you do not have the truth.

If you read any law book on cross-examination, there is a range of different areas upon which lawyers can cross-examine you, but they generally cover five broad areas of attack. The first challenge to any witness is in relation to qualifications and experience. One of the reasons I did a PhD was to look better in court – "Dr Watts" has more authority than "Mr Watts". I try not to play the qualification game, but from time to time I have been forced to play it. For example, I once had a solicitor ask: "Mr Watts, you shouldn't be able to answer that because you are not a doctor". I said: "Well, actually it's Dr Watts, and I can answer that because I am qualified in this area as a psychologist". Sometimes the game is more subtle. In one case in which I was involved, a social security overpayment (criminal) trial, I argued that my client was suffering from major depression. A cunning lawyer put to me: "Well you cannot prescribe medication for depression, can you?" I had to say "no" and he would not let me elaborate.

Another way that a lawyer will try to show that you are not adequately qualified is to break down your experience. This was illustrated in the earlier example about the indigenous father who killed his white wife, where the grandparents were fighting for custody of his children. These approaches are ploys and judges often see through them but, if you get shaken in the opening gambit, there is a greater chance that the lawyer will force you to crumble in your later evidence (where it really matters).

If you are a new graduate, a lack of experience can be a problem. If all else fails, go back to your qualifications, however, this may or may not be useful. I once spoke to a lawyer about a Family Court case in which a witness was a Psychologist Registrar who had done a Master's degree but was still in her first year of supervised practice. She was asked: "Have you got any experience in the area of attachment?" She gave a really good response: "I haven't worked with children but I have studied it at a theoretical level in my university degree". However, the judge said: "Next line of questioning, this witness is not qualified to answer questions of attachment". He was not going to accept her expertise because she had not worked with children.

Ethically, it is important to stay within your area of expertise, whether you are newly qualified or very experienced. You do not have to be an expert on everything. The court will afford you greater respect if you admit when you are being asked about subjects beyond your field of knowledge.

Historically, there has been a hierarchy in the weighting of the value of experts. In the past the evidence from a psychiatrist outweighed a psychologist, which outweighed a social worker. A counsellor would probably not have been considered to be qualified to give expert evidence. From the perspective of my own profession, psychology has done a good job in clawing back the distance. In Western Australia, I find that in many courts a good psychologist's report is generally equal to that of a psychiatrist's report. In a 1995 Victorian judgment (R v David Joel Whitbread) the court noted that once the question of medical treatment was put aside, psychologists were found to be equal and, depending on knowledge and experience, possibly better qualified than some psychiatrists in relation to the mental states and processes of the mind. Likewise, social workers are also gaining in credibility in court but still have some distance to go. In relation to other professions, similar issues of credibility are constantly being argued in court.

The practical reality is that there are some judges who have been around for decades who refer back to a time when psychiatrists were the only experts qualified to give evidence, and they do not think psychologists and social workers are worth having in court. On the other hand, there are some judges, especially the newer ones, who are only too happy to hear psychological evidence. Therefore, qualifications and the usefulness of an expert is not only case-specific but it is judge-specific. It is important to remember that good evidence is good evidence, even if you are newly qualified or from a different profession.

The second aspect the cross-examining lawyer is going to challenge is the perceived impartiality of the witness. They are going to try to show that you are biased. That is where the information contained in the first half of this book comes in. If you set yourself up to be as independent as possible, this attack will be minimised. What they want to argue is that you are biased, subjective, work for one side, and are only saying positive things to protect your client. You have a choice. You can either argue that you offer an independent opinion, or limit your evidence to fact.

If you are in a service role, one way to handle it is to agree with the bias, acknowledge the limits of your position and only provide evidence of fact. "Yes, I was representing my client's position. I understand there are two sides to every story and I accept that I only have one side. However, in seeing that one side, I have observed the following ...". Rather than give an opinion you give factual evidence based on observations. The alternative is to try and give opinion evidence by minimising biases.

Preventing attacks on your objectivity should be managed by the little things you did along the way. For example, when were you paid for writing the report? I try to get paid before I release the report. This is for two reasons: you get paid because everyone wants to see the report but, more importantly, you can say: "They paid for my time, they did not pay for my opinion. I was paid before my opinion was released".

The third area of challenge is to the factual basis of your material. This is the material upon which you have based your evidence. They are going to start knocking holes in the observations, test data, historical information and interview material. If your assessment can be shown to be inadequate, then your findings might be seen as questionable. Once again, a well structured methodology and a clearly written report is the best defence against this attack.

Unfortunately, the rules of evidence are complex and the legal profession has the upper hand in challenges to the factual basis. For example, I once interviewed a 19-year-old girl whose uncle had allegedly sexually molested her when she was a 13-year-old. I also interviewed the uncle. In the Family Court report I offered an opinion about the likelihood of abuse and the risk the uncle posed to another child. At the trial the uncle was not called as a witness (a critical oversight by the lawyers) and the girl became so upset that her evidence was terminated by agreement. When I gave evidence I had to disregard what each of these witnesses had told me during the assessment, because the judge could not test their evidence. After leaving out the interviews with the perpetrator and victim, there was not much upon which to base a risk assessment. This may not be perceived as fair but, as explained earlier, the court process is not about our everyday sense of fairness; it is about a set of rules applied to a particular case.

The fourth area of challenge in the cross-examination is to identify defects in the reasoning process. The opposing lawyer now wants you to justify your conclusions on the basis of the evidence. It is important that you have outlined the logic you used to come up with your opinion. In effect, the approach should be shown in the data; how you reached this particular inference and what alternatives there were. In the same way that the judge has to provide reasons for their decision, the court needs a reason for your opinion.

This is an area where many professionals become unstuck. They outline what they did and found, then offer opinions without explaining the link. The court needs to understand your line of logic in reaching a conclusion. So you need to show A – B – C, not A – C. They have to see the middle step B – the inferences. It is not enough to say "it is my opinion" unless you can explain why that opinion came about. A colleague, who was the court expert in a Family Court matter, recently had a judge refuse to accept his report as evidence. The judge argued that he appeared to have made appropriate enquiries and had reached opinions. However, the colleague had not explained how he had reached the opinions, so the judge could not accept the report. The trial was halted and my colleague had to rewrite the report.

The final aspect of the cross-examination is not an attack, although it may seem that way. This is where the lawyer draws out evidence helpful to their own client. In most cases lawyers do not want to totally exterminate professional witnesses. What they want to do is to get the evidence they need. They will just dissect you and cut out the pieces they do not want! In effect they are going to say that you may be inadequately qualified, highly biased and that you made a whole bundle of mistakes in collecting your evidence, but you at least got these aspects right about their client!

The court is also very respectful and what you will find is that as an expert witness, giving opinion evidence, the court will credit you with a bit more respect than if you were just giving evidence of fact. If you were a layperson, it is probable that you would have a harder time – the lawyer would be happy to totally exterminate you. The court does have a certain respect for experts and professional people.

I would point out that the lawyer in court may not follow the order given above but, in any good cross-examination, I would expect to see aspects of each of those five strategies. Hopefully, by understanding what the lawyer is trying to achieve, it will not seem so personal.

Re-examination

After the intense pressure of the cross-examination the first lawyer is able to re-examine you. They are not allowed to introduce new information, but they can do a bit of damage control on issues raised during the cross-examination. Usually, this is quite brief and is over before you know it.

The process explained above is the standard case where there are two sides. However, there are times when there may be more than two sides. I was once involved in a Supreme Court trial in which five men had been charged with rape. Each man had legal representation. This meant a cross-examination by counsel for each of the four parties and one by the public prosecutor. Similarly, there are often more than two sides in Family Court matter. A mother and father may both have legal representation, the children may have had their own lawyer appointed to them, there might be some grandparents who also have a lawyer, and a welfare agency may be an intervener. It can get complicated, but the procedures are basically the same.

In certain circumstances a judge may ask questions of the witness directly. In criminal and civil courts it is unlikely that the judge would ask many questions as the process is more adversarial, but they might direct the lawyers to ask certain questions. In the Family Court, and in some children's courts, they have a different sort of mandate (usually because they are based on an enquiry model) so it is not uncommon for a Family Court judge to ask specific, and at times biting, questions. Usually, after questioning by a judge, the lawyers are asked if they want to clarify anything, as the judge is not usually allowed to introduce new information.

The Judgment

After the testing has taken place, the judge or magistrate usually makes findings of fact about the information given and then applies the relevant law to those facts. This process is called a judgment. Judgments may be handed down immediately after all of the evidence has been heard but in many cases the decision is reserved until the judge can review all the information and formulate reasons for the decision. These situations may result in the judgment being handed down weeks or months after a trial.

Anyone who has studied statistics will quickly realise that the concept of a judgment makes sense. In statistics there are probability levels. Generally, this is whether the alpha level is set to .01 or .05. Underlying the theory of probability is the knowledge that we cannot test if something is true, we can only test how likely or not the result occurred by chance. The same process applies in court. A judge rarely knows if something really happened as he or she was not there. The judge can only infer the likelihood that an event took place with a degree of certainty.

In the criminal court, the standard of proof is called "beyond reasonable doubt". The jury (or judge sitting without a jury) has to be really sure something happened. The risk of making the wrong decision is severe because someone could lose their right to freedom. Hence, the standard is set to a higher level – it is better to have ten guilty individuals go free than to lock up one innocent person. While the public does not like the concept of guilty people going free, it actually addresses the statistical problem of Type I and Type II errors.

In other courts, the cost of a mistake is seen as less severe than the loss of freedom. My understanding is that in almost every other court (that is, courts other than criminal courts) the standard of proof is based on the "balance of probabilities". The judge has to be more sure than not, that something is true. In a crude sense, they need to be 51 per cent sure that it happened, rather than 99 per cent sure in the criminal court.

The different probability levels can create interesting dilemmas. For example, in a case before the Family Court a father was alleged to have sexually abused his stepdaughter. He was charged by the police and went to trial in the District Court. After hearing the evidence the District Court judge found him "not guilty". However, on the basis of the Family Court trial, he was found to be an unacceptable risk to the child. In effect this meant that he had been found found by the court to be "guilty". The man was upset because he felt he had been tried twice for the same crime. From a legal perspective, underlying this issue, acquittal does not mean innocence. It means that the requisite standard of proof had not been met.

As a layperson we want to believe that the court is about truth. We want the guilty people locked up and the innocent to go free. We want right to prevail. As stated previously, a court is not about absolute truth; it is about law and rules of evidence leading to justice.

Key Points

- Three sets of variables underpin credibility: expertise, trustworthiness and dynamism.

- Going to court consists of being sworn in, examined-in-chief, cross-examined and re-examined. After the lawyers present their closing submissions, a judge provides the reasons for their decision (a judgment).

- Cross-examination should be prepared for with the same rigor that you'd use to complete an exam. The better the preparation, the better the evidence.

- Expect that the cross-examination will examine: your qualifications and experience; biases in your approach; your methodology; the factual bases you relied upon; explanations of how the inferences operate; and then draw out information helpful to their own case.

- There are various ploys used by lawyers. If you spend too much effort trying to outsmart the lawyers, you may come across badly. Focus on truth, facts and reasoning and you will do better.

- If errors and weaknesses are shown up in your evidence, acknowledge them and move on.

In the Witness Box

Beginning with some of the fundamentals, it is important to understand that the lawyer or barrister in court is there to draw out evidence for the judge. The lawyer asks the questions but the answer is for the judge – you are addressing your remarks to the judge or magistrate, not to the lawyer. This is an awkward process for the inexperienced witness, because we are used to looking at the person asking the questions. As a novice witness you will make eye contact with the lawyer, whereas you really need to break that eye contact and look up at the judge.

What should a witness look for when looking at the judge? There are basically three variations: if the judge looks interested, talk more; if the judge looks bored, talk less;

if the judge has gone to sleep, keep talking and what you say will be on the transcript! With the advent of computers a judge may type rather than look at the witnesses. The same observation skills apply: if the judge is typing fast, keep talking; if the judge is typing slowly, they may either have lost interest or your evidence is not helpful.

The lawyer is not allowed to lead a witness to say things; they can only ask questions for you to be drawn out. As they can only ask questions, they cannot make statements. They may ask closed questions, which get a yes or no response, or they may ask open questions (for example, "Tell me about ..."). The examination-in-chief will consist of more open questions, while the cross-examination will consist of more closed questions. Experienced lawyers get very good at saying "is it not so" at the end of statements to turn it into a question.

There's an old legal adage: "never ask a question if you do not know the answer". A lawyer needs to be very careful with the questions they ask you, because they may get answers they do not want. It is important to remember that they may not want you to answer too many questions in case you say something unexpected.

As a quick aside, while talking about answering questions, it is important to understand that the little microphone in the witness box is not normally there to amplify sound; it is to record the things you say. This is the official record of the proceedings of the court from which a transcript will be produced. Therefore, it is important to speak clearly and into the microphone. In some courts the sound is amplified as well as recorded, because some witnesses speak more quietly when they are nervous.

If I were to run training courses for lawyers I would include a few fundamental tips on how to deal with expert witnesses ("Winning advocacy" by Selby and Blank (2004) is an excellent resource to help understand how an advocate's technique can affect cross-examination). The following principles (or tips) are those I'd include in a training session for lawyers:

Tip Number 1 – Being nice is much easier than being nasty. Among those who have not appeared in court before, there is an expectation that lawyers will be aggressive in their manner. One of the most effective Queen's Counsel before whom I have given evidence has been nicknamed "everyone's friend". He is seductively nice to the witnesses, so much so that they are lured into giving him the answers he wants. Judges in Australian courts will in general not tolerate lawyers who use an aggressive, table thumping, yelling at witnesses approach, which you might see on television. It happens occasionally, but not very often.

On the other hand, if you as a witness get nasty towards the lawyers, you will lose your credibility because the court expects respect from you. The court tends to protect itself. If someone is being nasty to you, do not respond in the same way. We should be the masters of our emotions and reactions. You should use the strategy of maintaining your calmness in the face of a difficult lawyer. However, they may well be trained to be nice.

Tip Number 2 – Cross-examination requires a different approach. If the questions asked of the witness during examination-in-chief are discreet, then during the cross-examination the questions can be bold. The first examination is typically the friendlier one and usually includes more open questions. The cross-examination is where a witness will be controlled, to prevent the witness from going down unexpected paths. As a lawyer, part of the job is to ensure control of the witness.

Tip Number 3 – Lawyers read witnesses. Good cross-examiners watch a witness for signs of change. They are not staring down the witness, but their aim is to recognise any change in language or tone or body language. A really good lawyer is able to look for the subtle things.

The Game Plan of Lawyers

In addition to training lawyers in general approaches to questioning styles, I would also introduce them to the concept of having a game plan or strategy. Selby and Blank (2004) note:

Courtroom success means a well thought through game plan, for just the same reason as other high level competition. Without a plan there is no capacity to respond to changing conditions, to recognise and take advantage of openings, to use your material efficiently or measure your progress and gauge what is your next best move (p. 20).

This is something that has only become clear to me in the last few years. I would prepare my report, recognise the "holes" and be prepared for the lawyers to ask about them. The lawyers would then ask something completely different – things I believed were irrelevant. The reason they asked something different is because as lawyers they have a plan about what they are trying to do, what they are trying to achieve. Selby and Blank break it down into several component parts.

A lawyer will have a case theory of what they are trying to achieve. In a particular case they know which angle they want to take. Selby and Blank talk about having a motif, like a short phrase that sums up the essence of the case. For example, if the parties to a case are suing a builder because they have had a kitchen renovation go wrong, their lawyer might argue the case for them using the phrase "dreams gone wrong". It was not the fact that the kitchen renovations went wrong, it was their dreams that were shattered. They want compensation for their lost expectations, not just for the job that was not carried out properly – they want psychological compensation. When the case gets difficult the lawyer will keep coming back to that basic phrase.

The game plan stems from the motif. How they are going to tackle this case on the strength of that plan? The plan sets the direction and acts like a keel on a boat by steadying the direction of the examination. This then underpins what they are doing and determines what they will and will not ask of the witnesses.

When you understand that the lawyers have set a plan, in some cases established many months before the trial, it begins to make sense (that is, why you may have prepared your evidence about what you think they may ask, but they do not ask those questions). In the alternative, they ask a whole lot of questions which you never expected, because they are trying to achieve their particular angle. If you talk to the briefing lawyer, or courtroom barrister, they might tell you the theory of the case, but most of them will not because they do not want you to give particular responses.

Handling the Questions

As described earlier, appearing in court has been likened to a duel, except you have a very short sword. It is important that you understand your sword and how to use it to your advantage.

For example, you can ask for time to process information, especially new information. If someone gave me a document

I had not read before, I would have a look at it and say that I need seven or eight minutes (assuming it was short) to read the document. I would then ask whether I should read it in the stand or whether the court will adjourn. It is up to the court to decide whether or not to adjourn, or sit and wait for you to read the document. If you read the document while in the witness box and everyone is waiting for your response, you need nerves of steel. I have no qualms about sitting and reading through a document, because I am there to give an opinion based on the evidence. So you should not feel pressured just because you have a judge, a couple of lawyers and others sitting waiting for you to read it. Take your time and read it thoroughly because, if you do not, you will be in trouble.

Perhaps the most useful sword skill comes from knowing exactly what your role is in court. Once mastered, you will give evidence in an effective fashion. The "ultimate issue" was discussed earlier. A great witness is one who keeps within their expertise, leaving the ultimate issue for the judge to decide. For example, in a Family Court case I may be asked, in light of some new information, where the children should live. My response would be to look at the judge and say: "Your honour has heard three days of evidence, it no longer matters where I think the children should live". Usually the judge will agree and the next question is asked. Even when asked to answer, my response indicates that I respect the role of the judge.

One of the areas in which inexperienced people in court come unstuck the most is with respect to responses to hypothetical questions. When asked a hypothetical, if you do not know what you are doing, you may end up arguing the point. If someone says: "Suppose for example, X happened". You might respond: "Well, I found no evidence that X happened", and then you get into a defensive mode.

If you see yourself as a scientist, there to assist the court, then your role is to provide that information. If provided with a hypothetical, you integrate the information and give an opinion; do not get defensive. You could say: "I found no evidence suggesting that to be the case but, if that was the case, this is how my opinion would be affected". It is critical to understand that someone may have said earlier in the proceedings that X did happen, but you may be the only person in the room unaware of this fact. Similarly, even if X was found not to have happened, the judge hearing the evidence may find your assistance helpful.

Hypotheticals can come in different forms. If a lawyer asks you a general question, it is important to clarify what they are talking about, otherwise you may make an assumption about something that is too broad to highlight. So, the more specific the new facts can be put to you, the better able you will be to give an opinion. If you are going to give an opinion it has to be based on something. You might find that one lawyer will put something to you, somebody will disagree with it, and then the judge will have his or her say. They might debate exactly what was said, and then the comment will be put to you. In this process even the lawyers might negotiate what the facts may have been.

This is nothing to do with someone trying to trick you. It is all about you assisting the court to understand different scenarios, and the better you can handle that, the better your overall evidence will be. If the hypothetical is outrageous, you can disagree with it, but if it is plausible, then roll with it and let the judge decide what the real facts are and which one of your opinions is going to work.

Questions about whether something is "possible" are less direct forms of a hypothetical. This is a little different to other forms of hypothetical in that the lawyers may be trying to raise doubt. The expert will be presented with alternative facts and asked whether it is possible. Of course anything is possible, but what you have to do is give a reasonable degree of likelihood and explain your reasons, because that is what your evidence will be based on.

Another common scenario to be aware of is the use of "yes or –no" questions and knowing how to counter them. As discussed earlier, the lawyer wants to control the witness. The witness needs to avoid being controlled. If asked a yes or no question, there are four levels of responses I would make.

The first level of response is to try to give an explanation prior to answering with a yes or no. In normal speech patterns you would answer: "Yes, but ...", however, in this case you would answer: "But ... yes". The second level of response is to argue that the question is too complex for a simple "yes or no" answer. Make sure that you are looking at the judge when you say this. The third level of response is to state that: "To answer with a yes or no response would be misleading to the court". If these three responses are not successful, the final strategy is not to get angry, but to overemphasise the "yes or no" responses in a way that indicates you are not committed to the response. This alerts the judge (or jury) and the briefing lawyer that it is not something you are committed to.

You should be very wary of a strategy in which a lawyer quotes something you have said, and then asks you to agree that it is what you have said. There is nothing wrong with agreeing with what you have said, but you need to listen to it very carefully, because lawyers will often try to put a spin on your words. Their goal is to shift what you have said to suit their purpose. In the process, they may misquote you, or they may give you the truth of what you have said in part only. If you are not careful, those little things can really set you up. This is a process in which you can walk away from the court and really feel that your evidence was misunderstood or twisted, because they have got you to agree to the things they put to you. The key point is: never agree to something unless it is exactly what you mean. If a lawyer puts something to you, and you do not quite agree with it, then reframe it until you both agree that is what you say and mean.

Similarly, evidence you have given previously, whether at another trial or in a research paper you have written, may be cited to you. Listen carefully to ensure that it is what you have said and that it is in context. Any quote taken out of context can have a negative impact upon you. Do not be afraid to ask for clarification.

When you do court work, you will sometimes have personal questions thrown at you, for example, "do you have children?", or "are you married?". It is usually a self-represented litigant who will ask these questions, not a lawyer. There are three types of responses to questions of this nature. First, the judge will say that it is an inappropriate question. Second, one of the lawyers will object, saying that you cannot answer the question. Finally, it is left to you to deal with the question. My main line of defence is: "I am here to give a professional opinion, not a personal opinion". Sometimes the judge might say that the question should be answered anyway, as it is a question which all of the witnesses have been asked. You should just answer factually and move on.

Some professionals have skeletons in their closets. That is, past actions have taken place and are now potentially bad. For example, if a tax accountant has been barred from practice for inappropriate returns to the tax department will have some serious problems in court. If you have a large flaw in your character resulting from past actions, avoid court if possible. If you have to go to court, the judge will in most cases not allow the situation to get personal. If the issue of your past action comes up, and you have to answer, acknowledge the problem and move on. Do not get into a big debate. If the issue is raised and you try to hide it or get defensive, you are going to dig yourself into a hole. In summary, take your time before you answer to give the judge or the other lawyer time to interject. When you do answer, provide the facts and move on.

Key Points

- The lawyers may ask the questions but your evidence is for the judge, not the lawyers.

- A lawyer may only ask questions, they are not allowed lead you.

- Being nice is a strategy that is just as disarming as being aggressive. Avoid being lulled into a false sense of security by a lawyer who is overly nice to you.

- If the lawyer is aggressive, do not become defensive or aggressive in return as it can damage your credibility.

- When you understand that the lawyers have set a "game plan", based on their theory of the case, it makes it easier to understand why certain questions are asked (and not asked).

- A credible witness knows their rights in court. The right to understand what is being asked, and the right to have time to contemplate questions and new material are important tools.

- Hypothetical questions are not simply tricks to get you to agree to things that are not true. They are an opportunity to show your worth to the court by being able to provide intelligent alternatives based on differing fact patterns.

- Ensure that you listen carefully to, and only agree with, quotes from your evidence. A good lawyer will get you to agree with partial truths by altering the meaning of what you have said.

6

Going to Court

Considerations for Court

This chapter addresses some of the practical issues involved in going to court. As explained throughout this book, the material presented only provides insight into a generic approach. Make sure you find out the specifics of any local protocols for a particular court.

Court Dates and Times

Lawyers work on the principle of billable units of time. This means that they do not want to do things that are unnecessary as it wastes their valuable time. If they are preparing for a court appearance they will read the entire brief of documents close enough to the event in order to remember the material. If they read the documents a month in advance, they have to read them a second time just before the appearance, which uses up precious time and costs someone money. The implication of this is that the legal team will study the case close to the time for appearing in court resulting in a mad flurry of activity at what seems to us to be the last minute. They read the material and find gaps in the case so they seek further reports and other information. As it is now close to the court date, it means that everything is urgent. Recently, a lawyer telephoned me on a Wednesday to request a report by the Friday!

In the procedural rules of court, there are periods of time within which documents have to be filed before a trial. Typically, all of the parties send their information in at various periods determined by the court, such as 30 days, 28 days, or 21 days beforehand (obviously it depends upon the rules of the particular court). This may be the first time that both sides see all of the reports and documents. This allows them to decide whether to settle the case, because they can now see how weak or strong their case may really be. Often during the last few days before a trial, and sometimes even during a trial, the parties reach agreement.

Consequently, trials often fall through at the last minute. In my experience, for every three trials I diarise in my planner, two will settle. I therefore have to operate like the lawyers and save my preparation to near the trial date. I may not charge billable minutes but my time is my business and it is not reusable!

You should not become too anxious about a pending trial, as more often than not a trial will not go ahead. This does not mean that you should not collect together the material in preparation; it means you do not need to spend too long studying it prior to the time you need to give evidence.

For example, if I am unsure of the current literature on a particular topic I may pay a student to research the topic, or I may search the Internet, but I do not study the material in detail until the last few days.

When you receive instructions for going to court, make sure that you find out when they want you to attend. Professional people are often "interposed" (put in by agreement, even if it is contrary to the normal order of proceedings) at a convenient time. If you are an officer of the court, such as a court counsellor or, in some jurisdictions, a public servant, you may not have a choice. You may be required to attend when the court stipulates.

If you have a choice, there are preferable appearance times. Start times vary depending upon the court, but somewhere between 9.30am and 10.15am is usual. Occasionally, a court will start earlier. If you can, see if you can give your evidence first thing in the morning. I find that as the day goes on, the likelihood of the court running late increases. However, if I cannot be the first witness of the day, being the first witness after lunch is not bad. Timeslots like 11.30am and 3.30pm are almost always going to run late so bring something to read. Even worse, if they do not finish with you before lunch or before the court adjourns for the day, you may have to wait until after the lunch break or come back the next day.

Most judges are reasonable people who will try to accommodate the professional person, especially if they are aware of special circumstances. I have been involved in cases where they have altered times to accommodate me. For example, on one occasion I was in the country. The judge asked if I could give my evidence on the next day as they were not likely to get through the other witnesses before 5pm and she wanted me to give my evidence last.

I explained that my wife was at home with nine-week-old baby twins and that I had booked to fly back at 8pm that night. The judge kindly offered to have the court sit until 7.30pm, if necessary, to finish the evidence and get me on the flight home. I have seen judges sit through lunch breaks, start court early, and go over time to ensure that my evidence was finished (so I did not have to come back).

On the other hand, I have also had judges stop at 4.30pm on the dot and require that I return for just ten minutes the next day. It depends on the judge, but if you do not let your needs be known then there is no chance of you getting your needs met. So if you have a special need, let the briefing lawyer know or speak to the judge and see what happens. It is important to express your appreciation when they do vary the process to accommodate you as they are not obliged to do so – they can make you sit outside the courtroom until they need you!

In some states the Family Court has a system of a "not before date". For example, if a trial is not to commence before the 14th April, it could commence on the 15th, the 16th or the 17th. The reason for the "not before date" is to reduce the need for judges to sit around idle when there is a backlog of cases. As many Family Court matters settle, the system needs a way of dropping settled cases without leaving gaps, so pending trials are banked up. Civil trials tend to have a specific date and that date is fixed for many months.

Before setting a trial date, the lawyers should approach their witnesses and ask if there are any times when they are not available to give evidence. The usual request is something like: "Can you please advise us of your unavailable dates for the months of ...?" Once advised, they should then ensure that the trial is held at a time when you are available. Obviously, unavailable dates are about substantial absences such as interstate trips, major training events and the like. I generally do not worry about single days when I may not be available as usually it is possible to work around it (unless the matter is a short-listed hearing of only one day). It is when I am not available for two or more days that I consider listing myself as unavailable for a trial.

Giving Evidence

Most lawyers will want to know what you are going to say. As stated earlier, one of the principles of good cross-examination is never ask a question to which you do not know the answer. Therefore most briefing lawyers (the one who got you involved in the first place) will want to talk to you about your evidence. I always try to talk to the lawyer about what they will ask me. Do note that there are protocols relating to what a lawyer may be able to tell you (and even whether they can talk to you at all). The general rule is that a briefing lawyer is the one who can talk to you. If you are subpoenaed, there may be no briefing lawyer.

There are two main ways of talking to the lawyer. I either telephone the briefing lawyer and/or trial barrister a few days in advance, or I ask to meet them half an hour before I give evidence (I meet them outside the courtroom). I generally make notes of what they are going to ask me so I can think about my responses. You should realise that they will also take note of your answers to see if it is worth asking those questions on the day. Do not feel intimidated by this process, as it is a "warm up" for when you get to court. On more than one occasion a lawyer has telephoned me to request a list of questions I wish to be asked. Better still, I have been asked to look at another professional's report and provide a list of questions for the lawyer to ask. This type of request is rare, but interesting. Do not be disappointed if they do not use your questions as their game plan may relate to issues different to the ones you've identified.

It is important to remember that in the lead up to the trial, the lawyers have had access to all of the information and they have probably tried to reach some sort of settlement. All of the documents have been filed so they know what the other side has. After they have been to the conciliation meetings, they know what the sticking points are. If they can tell you what the other side is going to ask you, you can prepare in advance. Over time I have come to realise that what I think may be relevant to the trial is not necessarily what the lawyers consider relevant. Therefore I will ask my briefing lawyer what the other side may want to ask me.

If you ask this type of question be careful about privilege. As described earlier, there are rules of law that protect communications between a briefing lawyer and client. A lawyer may not be able to answer certain questions. How much the lawyer can tell you depends upon the nature of your involvement. As a court expert you may be told quite a lot, while as a subpoenaed witness you may not be told anything at all. My advice is ask; it is the lawyer's job to know the rules about what, from the court's perspective, may be privileged.

In terms of etiquette, I do not seek information from parties who have not briefed me at some point in the process. I certainly would not contact an opposing lawyer or barrister to ask what they are going to ask me. If a party is self-represented, the situation is much harder. This is a common problem in the Family Court where cases may take place with one or both parties appearing without a lawyer. However, there are people who represent themselves in many different types of court cases. Having discussions with someone who does not have legal representation can open you up to all sorts of problems and is best avoided wherever possible.

Another important consideration involves the timing of your discussions with lawyers. Once you have started to give evidence in court, you must not talk to anyone about your evidence (unless you are expressly told that you are permitted to do so). This applies whether you have a five-minute adjournment, overnight breaks in the evidence, or a trial split over weeks or months. Your evidence must be kept pure, which is part of the reason why witnesses are not allowed to sit in court until after they have given evidence. Once your evidence has been completed, unless otherwise stated, you can talk to various lawyers again (within the bounds of confidentiality, ethics etc.).

Read All Your Information

One of my worst experiences in court occurred before a Family Court trial judge. It was a complicated trial. The trial was underway and I was to give evidence on the Thursday. On the Tuesday, a courier dropped off a large wad of documents, which proved to be the grandmother's diary relevant to this case. For a number of months she had had the young child in her care and had recorded everything. When I received the documents, I was having a very busy week (full days, evening meetings, etc.). On the Thursday before court, I got up early and I read all of the affidavits that had been filed, all of my notes, my report, and other reports, but I only glanced through the diary.

I went to court. The trial started really well but one of the lawyers said something like: "Dr Watts, in the diary provided by the grandmother ...", and I said: "Well, I have only just scanned it". The judge then stopped, the lawyer stopped, everyone looked at the judge, and the judge said something to the effect: "I consider that [to be] a very important piece of information. Are you saying, Dr Watts, that you have not read it?" I had to say: "Yes, Your Honour". After what seemed like a huge pause he said: "You've got two choices. I can stop the trial now and resume it tomorrow after you have read it, or you can continue and give your evidence without having read this very significant piece of information", or words to that effect. The judge then adjourned for lunch while I considered my decision. I went to a lawyer's office nearby, locked myself in and spent the next hour and a quarter reading all of the documents I could possibly read. I then went back to court and explained what I had done. The judge sort of went "humph" and the trial continued.

In his judgment, there were parts of my evidence the judge liked, but he was damning of the way I had dealt with the diary. While it was difficult for me to have read that material in the time I had, the judge was correct in his view that I should have read the material before giving evidence upon it. The moral of that story is that if material is sent to you, read it. It was an awful experience and one that could have been avoided.

Bringing Material to Court

One of the common questions I get asked is: "What can I bring to court with me?" There may be an argument about what you can actually use at the time, but it is important to bring certain things. The most obvious item is the complete file related to the case. It is very rare that you will not be permitted to refer to your original notes and assessment data. The deciding factor for the judge is whether there is a link between the recording of the notes and the event in question. If you ask to look at the notes to "refresh your memory" then it will probably be allowed as the implicit assumption is that the notes contain the contemporaneous information needed to assist recall.

When you look though your notes, make sure they are in order and you know approximately where to find things. The use of small stick-on tags is very handy to highlight particular documents of significance. If you are obsessive, you could colour-code them to separate reports from test data and observations. Be aware, however, that anything you take into court and rely upon during your evidence can become part of the court records, so it is important that you do not take anything that you are not prepared to surrender.

I take a folder I call my court file. The file is of course black because I want a formal look. In it I have copies of my current curriculum vitae, a full résumé, and various items of potential use. I have reliability and validity scales for some common psychological tests (which I have never actually used but are there "just in case"). I have some literature on a variety of key relevant issues. I also take relevant references, such a DSM-IV (a handbook on mental disorders – considered to be the industry standard).

I take this court file into court with me and if I am asked a really curly question I say: "I have some information with me, can I refer to it?" I have about an 80 per cent approval rate in the Family Court and 60 per cent in criminal courts. Different courts have slightly different rules but, if you have it and can use it, why not? Having the file with me also gives me something to read while I am waiting for court to commence.

A helpful hint is that if you have something relevant,

such as criteria for a particular personality disorder, medical diagrams, or other material, make at least four copies for your file. You will look very professional if you have multiple copies to share around. If you had only one copy, you may have to wait while the clerk goes to another room to photocopy the document (and everyone remains silently waiting for their return).

Key Points

- Expect legal cases to consist of periods of rushed activity prior to deadlines, punctuated by seemingly long periods of inaction.

- Most trials settle at the last minute. Do not over-invest your energies in early trial preparation.

- If you have a choice about the time at which you can give your evidence, generally the times for the first witness of the day and the first witness after lunch are the most likely to run to schedule.

- Meet with the lawyer or barrister prior to court if appropriate and possible. Find out what they are going to ask you. Listen to their questions, but know they are also listening to your answers!

- Once you have commenced your evidence, during any breaks or adjournments, do not to speak to anyone about your evidence until the court says that they have finished with you.

- Read all of the information provided, especially your report and original case notes.

- Bring your notes and other information to court. Expert witnesses are often allowed the right to review a "memory aid".

Courtroom Procedures

Basic Etiquette

Arriving at the court early is a good start. If you arrive late, you will not be composed, calm, or have time to discuss things with the briefing lawyer. If you are very late, the judge may already have a negative view of you for wasting everyone's time. Therefore, in the larger cities, ensure that you allow adequate time for traffic and parking.

If you have not been to court before, arrive half an hour early and ask for the lawyer to give you a quick look around. Alternatively, there are now web sites that enable you to have a virtual tour of a courtroom (see, for example, the web site of the WA Department of the Attorney-General – http://www.justice.wa.gov.au).

Courts vary slightly in design but they have basically the same format. The judge generally sits higher than everybody else. In front of the judge is usually the judge's associate. There is a "bench" (that is, a table) where the lawyers and their clients sit facing the judge. At the back of the court is the gallery where spectators and people who have finished giving their evidence sit. At one side of the courtroom, near the judge, is the witness box where you will give evidence. Generally, there is also an usher who sometimes sits on the side or sometimes roves around to different places. In many courtrooms there is a little booth where a person monitors the taping equipment for recording the court proceedings.

Your entry to court will be at one of two main times. The court is either waiting to start or is already in progress. If the court proceedings have not started, you can walk in and introduce yourself to the lawyers (if possible, exchange pleasantries to both sides but certainly to the briefing lawyer). Alternatively, at least meet the usher and introduce yourself. If the court is ready for your evidence, it is generally acceptable to sit at the back of the court until called (unless there are arguments about your evidence in which case wait outside until called). If the court is in progress, it is normal for a witness to wait outside.

Even though you may appreciate that court is a "game" and you can speak to the various lawyers, your client may not see the court in that way (and therefore may not like to see you talking to the "enemy"). For this reason, ensure that you do not become flippant or casual in court, even if you know the lawyers well.

I suggest that you look into the courtroom before entering (most courtrooms have a small window in the door) to ensure that there is neither a witness talking nor a lawyer standing. If you are a witness it is not appropriate to enter unless you have the permission of the court to do so. However, if you do have permission, and a lawyer is standing, then it is okay to enter the court quietly. If the court is in session, open the door, catch the eye of the usher (without entering the court), and then wait outside until called.

Court Rules are Formal

The legal profession is guided by a variety of rules and customs established over several hundred years. One custom or protocol in general use in all courts is that of bowing to the judge. This is more like a nod of the head than a gracious bow one might give to royalty. The bow is made each time the judge enters the court. Similarly, when you enter or leave the court, it is normal to pause briefly at the door and bow to the judge. No one will come after you for not doing it, but it looks professional if you do bow.

One rule, which is strongly policed, is that mobile phones must be turned off. In this age of technology, one of biggest breaches of etiquette you can commit in court is to allow your phone to ring. In some courts it is also considered rude to have your sunglasses on the top of your head so remember to take them off.

The use of correct titles in court is very important. An almost universal convention is that a judge is referred to as "your honour", and a magistrate is referred to as either "your worship" or, in some courts, "your honour". The terms "sir" or "madam" are commonly used when you talk to anyone in court. Lawyers should be called by their surnames with the title "Mr", "Ms", "Mrs" or "Miss". Children are generally referred to by their first names, but adults are referred to by their title and surname. In the Family Court, it may be possible to refer to the parties by their first names but, if you are not sure, the safest line is to err on the side of formality.

Your Rights in Court

As touched on earlier, you do have some, but not many, rights in court. You are entitled to be comfortable. For example, if you need a drink of water the usher will get you one. As it is common for someone to get a dry mouth when nervous, a drink is a good idea. Having a drink can also be used as a strategy if you feel that your composure is going. Pause to have a drink, then answer.

You also have the right to understand the question. If the question catches you off guard, take a few moments to think before answering. If the question reflects new information, it is possible, and indeed encouraged, for you to say: "Can I think about that for a few moments before answering?" If a question is long, it is possible to ask for it to be rephrased if you do not understand. If the question has multiple parts then ask that they be addressed one at a time. If a lawyer asks a particularly long question, simply asking for it to be repeated can be a good strategy – if a lawyer had not read the question from their notes, they may not be able to repeat it.

Hopefully, you will have remembered to go to the toilet before giving your evidence but if you need a toilet break it is appropriate to ask by using the politest terms possible. Be warned that the judge may choose to stop for lunch if it is nearly time, so if you have nearly finished your evidence, hang on! What starts as a five-minute stop may become an hour-and-a-half break.

I have also discovered through hard experience that you should never take medication you are not familiar with. Fortunately, my experience related to a mock trial for training purposes. I had a horrible head cold so I had taken a couple of anti-cold tablets and some cough mixture. As I was not used to the medication, and was not well, I became quite faint. If I had been trying to give evidence, and not reading a script, I would have had a real problem. If you are genuinely ill, please let the court know as early as possible and ensure you get a medical certificate to prove that you had a real illness. Calmative medications such as benzodiazepines are not recommended unless they are your usual prescription medication.

Demeanour

"Demeanour" is not a word commonly used by the health profession but is something a lawyer may use. The reason is simple. Demeanour is concerned with outward appearance. It fits with the legal principle of factual evidence being that which can be seen or heard.

The first aspect to developing the appropriate demeanour is your appearance. Look like an expert in dress and manner. Judges are not only listening to what you are saying, they are also looking at how you come across as you say it. I was once involved in a case in which another psychologist had been attacking my report, and I felt she had been quite personal in her attack. When I gave evidence, I was asked to comment on her critique of my report. Due to the emotion associated with the issue, I went on about her critique. An experienced barrister who had been present said to me afterwards: "Phil, why did you even go there? You should have just rolled your eyes back, given a big sigh and with a look of contempt so as to imply 'why bother with this woman?'" I am not sure I would be prepared to play the game to that level but that is how that barrister considered it should be played.

Demeanour from the aspect of dress is also important. Irrespective of how you look in your office, a court is formal. When I am in court, I always dress in a suit, unless I am called on an urgent and unexpected basis to give evidence (which in general should not occur). In some courts the dress expectations for female witnesses can be old-fashioned. I have heard of a female lawyer arriving in court dressed in trousers who was subsequently told to change. Hopefully, that was a rare event in these enlightened times. If in doubt, it may pay to discuss the local protocol with your lawyer. However, what is not in doubt is the need to power dress.

A calm presentation is important but this is not always easy to achieve in the high-stress environment associated with giving evidence in court. Anyone in the mental health area is likely to have received training in relaxation skills and anxiety management techniques. We teach these techniques to our anxious clients but when it comes time to go to court, we seem to forget how to apply the techniques to ourselves. Irrespective of your own training, if you are feeling anxious remember basic breathing techniques (such as breathing out slowly while thinking the word "calm"). You can also have a sip of water, or pause to think about an answer. It may help to remember that we do not want to remove all anxiety. The inverted U relationship between anxiety and performance means that an optimum level of arousal is needed to achieve peak performance.

Your demeanour should not extend to the point of being arrogant or defensive. I once had a case in which I was asked to watch a video I had taken to see if I agreed with a statement from my report that the girl was pointing to her vagina. On watching the video it was not clear whether the girl was pointing to her leg or her vagina. I tried the approach: "It doesn't matter what I think now, the video is here for the judge to decide". That did not wash with the judge and in his reasons for decision he said I was defensive. The lesson from the experience is that if you make a mistake, it is better to own up to it than become defensive. David Childs, a leading Perth Family Court barrister, advises: "If you have to give ground or make a concession, do so! It is not unusual for this to happen and it is better to make the concession rather than stick to a lost point".

Your demeanour should also reflect the position discussed earlier in relation to expert evidence. You are not advocating for a client but assisting the court.

You may on occasion be questioned about either a particular article or your knowledge of the literature in general. It is important that you do not let this fluster you. How you handle the question depends upon your knowledge of the literature. If it is an area in which you are clearly comfortable, it probably does not matter.

However, if they have referred you to an area which you should possibly have known about, but which you do not, then you are in serious trouble. If the case is potentially going to enter into a debate on the literature, I will usually ring a colleague who specialises in the area so that I can get a current review article of the key material relevant to the issue.

There are a few doctors, psychologists and social workers with law degrees practising as lawyers, so the unexpected can happen. They are probably the most dangerous people you could meet in court because they actually know what they are asking you about. Usually lawyers will ask a few half-hearted questions to see how you respond. If you flinch, they will go for the jugular. If you stand your ground, they will usually back off, especially when they get into areas such as testing. It is very easy to baffle them if you want to. I have stressed throughout this book not to use jargon, however, this is the one time when you can use jargon. For example, if told that a test is not valid, respond with: "Which type of validity are you referring to; construct, criterion, or some of the other forms of validity?"

Costing

Those in the public sector are likely to have to attend court for their normal pay. The department they work for may be able to claim the cost of the lost time but, if they do, the worker will not see the money. In private practice, the recommended fee set by professional bodies for court attendance is generally higher than the normal hourly rate. This is because attending court is considered to require additional expertise and the court attendance interferes with the normal running of the practice. For example, the APS recommends a rate of 1.5 times the standard fee.

The most common problems in regards to payment for attending court stem from a failure to recognise that you need to negotiate a fee for service PRIOR to attending court. Some courts may have prescribed payments for the attendance but most do not. There are more likely to be fee schedules for expert witnesses in areas such as workers' compensation. In these cases, local knowledge of costing is required. In other cases, the legal profession understands that your service should be reimbursed. However, it is not up to the lawyer to determine how much you should be paid.

I consider a request to attend court to be a contract that needs to be negotiated prior to providing the service. It is an issue which should be dealt with by writing to the lawyer who has requested your court attendance to confirm attendance times, fees and your cancellation policy. If it is in writing, then everyone knows where they stand and the lawyer can allow for the funds for your payment to be held in trust and, if necessary, they can vary the arrangement with you.

An interesting consideration for some professions is that of GST. While you should get specific advice from a tax accountant, my understanding of the general principle is that treatment by a doctor, psychologist or other medical professional is a GST-exempt service (although "counselling" may attract GST). Writing reports, providing an assessment specifically for court, and giving evidence are not considered "treatment" so they are subject to GST. Therefore, do not forget to include this in the costing.

A cancellation clause needs to be included in any arrangement, because often cases will settle at the last minute. The issue you need to work out is your timeframe for cancellation fees. I do quite a lot of court work so I try to be reasonable and flexible about cancellations and changes. My normal policy is to have a 24-hour cancellation period requiring 50 per cent of the expected costs. Another aspect of cancellation is in relation to timing changes, for example, when you have been requested to give evidence in the morning but your appearance is changed to the afternoon at short notice. Some professionals charge, while others just see it as part of the costs of going to court. The bottom line is that you should balance the need to be flexible in assisting the court against the costs to your practice.

In my confirmation letter I also provide a minimum block of time for my availability. In what is expected to be a straightforward appearance, I state that I am available to the court for a two-hour minimum attendance (whether waiting or giving evidence) plus travel time. In complex matters I often state three hours. I also indicate the per hour rate for each additional hour.

In the case of a country matter, I may only be in court for a short time but I have to charge for the time I am away from my practice. This may be a whole day plus travel expenses. It is especially important to determine travel arrangements and associated costs well in advance of the appearance date.

Increasingly, evidence may be given via telephone or video link-ups in country or interstate matters, or for minor witnesses (to avoid the inconvenience of waiting around at court). I prefer to give evidence in person so that I can manage the dynamics of court by observing the interaction, but I understand the need to balance the cost against my preference. If I am a central party in a complex matter I insist on giving evidence in person. If I am a minor party I may consent to giving evidence by telephone. If you are a professional who sees clients, I would recommend that you do not allow the court to ring you at their convenience. Set up an agreed time so that you do not have to interrupt a client's treatment. Ensure that you are paid to be available, not just for the time on the phone.

Another thing you need to think about is the cost of preparation. I charge my standard assessment rate for preparation time. There may be a dispute about what are legitimate aspects of preparation. I allow a small preparation charge to re-read the material in my file (it would be expected that I know this material already, so I do not believe it is appropriate to charge for a lot of this type of preparation). I charge an hourly rate to read anything else the lawyer sends me, including other reports and trial affidavits, especially if I have not seen this material before. I do not normally charge for researching the literature unless the lawyer has requested a review. Knowing the literature is part of the role of being an expert.

Key Points

- Arrive early for court. If the court is in session, wait outside. If the court is waiting to commence, enter the room and introduce yourself to the lawyers or barristers, preferably those on both sides of the dispute.

- Maintain professionalism and decorum at all times, especially in front of the clients or parties to the case as they may not understand the "game" aspect of the court process.

- Court protocol is formal in dress and manner. Ensure that you understand the rules. Dress as formally as you comfortably can.

- Avoid taking medications and other mind-altering substances when appearing in court. Genuine sickness is a reason not to attend court but ensure that you have medical evidence.

- Your demeanour should be professional, intelligent and calm. Nothing is too much trouble in assisting the court. Being friendly is not essential, but hostility will damage your credibility.

- Expert witnesses are entitled to fair reimbursement for attending court. Most problems with fees are avoided if experts advise their expected costs in advance.

Becoming a Better Expert

How do you become better in court?   The answer is through using your experiences in court to give you feedback, as well as seeking ideas from other sources.

Feedback

One of the most powerful sources of feedback is the cross-examination.   Lawyers ask questions because they did not understand a part of your report or they saw something as a weakness. After going to court consider a two-part debriefing process. Initially you will need to resolve your emotions resulting from being in court. Once you can put your wounded ego aside, and think about what the lawyers or barristers cross-examined you on, you will learn how they viewed your written evidence. In particular, the questions you were asked are the issues that the lawyers did not understand.

Another form of feedback arises from your report. If you go to court and have your report admitted into evidence, but the lawyers do not ask any substantive questions, consider your report to be well-written. Either the issues in your report were so clear that the lawyers have accepted the report, or they were so concerned about the implications they did not want to touch it! Both options, particularly the former, are a credit to the way in which you approached the task.

One of the most powerful sources of feedback can come from the end user of your information, the judge. After a trial, a judge makes a judgment in which he or she explains how they, as the ultimate user of the information, viewed the witnesses' credibility and how that related to the relevant law. Just as we are expected to explain the factual base and inferences upon which our reports are based, the judge is also required to explain the basis of his or her decision. This is called different things in different courts. For example, it may be called a "reason for decision" in the Family Court, or "sentencing remarks" in a criminal court. A judge needs to provide reasons so that, if their decision is appealed, a higher court can consider those reasons. A judgment may be given verbally in court, or it may be provided in writing. Most lawyers would not think to send a copy of a judgment to an expert witness, but they are usually only too happy to do so if requested. Various web sites provide copies of court judgments, which are available to the public. I generally ask the briefing lawyer to send me a copy. It is one of the few times that you will ever get direct feedback on the way in which a judge perceived your evidence.

Another source of information comes from the barristers who examined your evidence in court. If you ask them directly, or through the lawyer who briefed you, it may be possible to get some useful feedback. How much they say will depend partly on your relationship with them, and partly on their personality. Some may tell it as it really is, while others will simply give you platitudes.

Develop Your Skills

I have emphasised throughout this book that it is imperative that you learn the rules of the game to deal effectively with court. To be a better expert you need to keep improving by learning the rules.

As with all academic skills, reading the literature is a useful approach. In the appended reference list, I cite a few examples of books in different areas of medico-legal process. I would recommend that you be discerning in the material you study. There is a mountain of literature available, however, much of it is American. I am not against American literature, but it is important to note that America has a different legal system which can be much more adversarial. American legal television shows have coloured the perceptions of many Australian professionals on what court may be like. When watching the shows, there is a sense of vicious challenges, verbal insults, and tricks to trip up the expert. In Australia that may happen, but in my experience it is relatively rare. I have found that in general I have been treated with respect; not yelled at or berated as seen on television!

Professional associations generally provide information on dealing with courts. I am aware that the Australian Medical Association is proactive in informing its members of expert evidence issues. The psychology profession has been a bit tardy but recently there have been some good articles in the APS professional magazine "In Psych". These have included dealing with subpoenas, the new Family Court Guidelines, and giving evidence in court. I have listed several of these in the reference list and, if you have access to the members' section of the web site, the articles are located there.

Training in all aspects of the legal process is an area of

professional development that all professionals should receive. I heard recently that complementary medicine and para-medical areas are being called the "cash cows of the new millennium" in terms of litigation. The context of the comment came in a discussion in which it was said that medical doctors are becoming too well defended and are protecting their assets more effectively. Other related professions are seen as poorly defended and ill-prepared for dealing with lawsuits. If we do not want to be milked, it is essential that we help ourselves by seeking ongoing training and reading the literature. As stated earlier, the more you know the rules of the game, the better you can survive the experience.

For want of a better name, court coaching is a useful strategy for improving performance in court. Some colleagues who are to appear in court will call me to discuss the case in a supervision session. I am certain that all professions have people experienced and willing to assist the less experienced. As long as confidentially is carefully guarded, and dual roles avoided, this can be tremendously helpful. Similar to coaching, a session of debriefing with an experienced colleague after giving evidence is a useful way to help make an objective appraisal of the situation.

Underpinning the different methods listed above is to do whatever you can to improve your understanding of the legal system. It is important to realise that differing opinions are a necessary part of the adversarial system. It does not matter if you have an opinion different to that of your colleagues. What you have to ensure is that you have a sound opinion, based on good evidence. Judge Wisbey notes:

It is important that the expert avoid adopting the role of a trailblazer for untried or dubious theories. If the expert wishes to be adventurous (and perhaps that shouldn't be discouraged) it is important that he or she enunciates clearly the novelty of the view, and identifies any opposing views.

Learning From My Mistakes

Even the most experienced court professional, highly regarded within a profession, can have a bad day in court. In a case like that it is important to analyse what happened so that you can learn from your mistakes. I share the following example so that you can also learn from my mistakes because it highlights the point that, even with experience, nobody is infallible.

The following example is based on a Family Court case. Obviously, information about the family needs to be kept to very general, non-specific details as it is not appropriate to release sensitive case-identifiable information. I also stress that the following represents my interpretation of the events – if you asked the judge or the various lawyers involved, they would have a different perception.

The case involved an assessment of issues to do with the welfare of one boy aged about ten whose parents had separated when he was a baby. The parents had never seen eye-to-eye but had muddled through a combination of weekend and shared care arrangements. The father had been convicted of physically assaulting the boy some three years previously. He was not gaoled but had received a suspended sentence. He had resumed contact and gradually the mother let him look after the boy during the week while she looked after him at the weekend. The father had had a relationship break-up and the ex-girlfriend raised various allegations of psychological and emotional harm to the boy.

To my mind, the case started out as a very routine Family Court expert appointment. I was therefore in that all-important independent position and had the opportunity to do a full assessment, which had involved more time than my standard Family Court assessment. It was a case where, when I interviewed the father, his own description of a number of events was extremely alarming from a psychological perspective. Consequently, I did not have to rely on making interpretations from what other parties had told me, as his own evidence was a compelling indictment. There was also other independent evidence, such as a previous conviction for physically assaulting the child and evidence from a police officer to whom the father had reported similar views (unfortunately the policeman was not called to give evidence as a witness at the trial).

I wrote a report. In the report, because I thought it was a cut and dried scenario, I focussed on one particular episode of concerning behaviour, which would have alarmed anybody. However, as I thought it was such a clear-cut case, I did not consider my trial preparation as seriously as I should have. The lesson here is that there is never a routine case; approach all cases as if they are complex.

The father objected to my report, but certain recommendations had been followed. In particular, the child needed psychological counselling and the father needed a psychiatric assessment. The psychiatric report failed to find the same level of concern I had noted (I had argued the possibility of either a delusional disorder or personality disorder). The psychiatrist came back with a view that the father lacked "common sense" but was not psychiatrically ill or personality disordered. Unfortunately for me, I was not aware that the child had been referred to the recommended psychological counselling. I was provided with a copy of that report about ten minutes into my evidence! The court was adjourned for a short time to allow me to read the report, but I did not have time to think through the implications. I offered the opinion that there was a certain degree of agreement between our reports but, because of the way the other report had been written, that overlap did not come through. Herein lay one of my problems. For future reference, if I am aware that someone is providing treatment I follow-up well before the trial to see if a report is to be provided to the court.

As described earlier, two sides of an argument are put before a judge to help the judge discern the situation. In this particular Family Court case, the father had engaged a noted Queen's Counsel (QC). I had known this particular QC for a decade and he is an extremely good strategist (as one would expect from a QC). The mother, on the other hand, was unable or unwilling to finance legal representation and was representing herself. Consequently, at the trial, in terms of the adversarial process, the father had a major advantage. In a case like this, where one party has legal representation and the other does not, it puts tremendous pressure on the expert to not only give evidence, but also to help counterbalance the adversarial process. In other words, I could not count on a lawyer bringing out the other side of the story.

When it came time for me to give evidence, the trial was running ahead of time (quite unusual in my experience). I had to give evidence a day earlier than expected which meant that I had a rushed preparation, and had not considered the issues with any great preponderance. Another point to be learned is to ensure that your preparation is done early enough to deal with a case running ahead rather than behind time. Preparation is one of the most important keys for surviving court.

An unfortunate problem in the evidence base was that I

had been asked to talk to the principal of the school about the child. The principal had been quite negative about the father's situation. On the day of the trial the class teacher, not the principal, was called to give evidence. Her evidence was favourable to the father and different to the principal's. My factual basis had evaporated into hearsay. The lesson here is to avoid using external sources unless you know they will be cross-examined.

My survival in court depended on how I structured my evidence. Unfortunately, I made some errors in structuring the evidence in the report, which became evident in court. In the report I was so struck with one particular incident the father had described, I had not considered detailing a number of lesser incidents. When the QC successfully shifted the main incident from the classification of psychological abuse to labelling it "an inappropriate act", I was left in a precarious position. I had not documented enough evidence in my report to argue that there was a pattern of behaviour on the basis of one incident.

I compounded my problems by being too emotive. One particular statement I made created a lot of problems. I stated that a particular incident was "one of the worst examples of psychological abuse I had assessed in the Family Court". Unfortunately, by wording it like that, I was too emotive and, when the court labelled the incident an inappropriate act, I was seen to be extreme. Consequently, the importance of documenting patterns rather than just noting the extremes, as well as being emotively understated, became apparent from this experience.

The net result was that the judge had to resolve the difference between my report, the father's current evidence and the two other reports he had before him. From a judge's perspective, because of my emotive language, the most plausible explanation he had before him was the one proposed by the father's lawyer, and that was partly that the father had been nervous at the time of the appointment and, more damaging for me, that I did not like the father. The concept of me not liking the father makes a lot of sense from a judge's perspective. As a psychologist who assesses rapists, murderers, drug addicts and all sorts of other "undesirable" people, the concept of liking or not liking does not enter the equation. Therefore, my entire evidence was now viewed from the perspective of whether or not I had liked the person.

What I needed to be able to do in this particular case was present several other options for the judge. There were at least two other alternatives for the differences in our opinions. First, the father had the benefit of reading my report and seeing my reaction. He was an intelligent man. The psychiatrist had made some notes about possible anti-social personality features, so I could have put forward the position that the father did present badly with me, realised his mistake and cleaned up his act on the shorter appointment with the psychiatrist. Alternatively, I could have argued along the lines that when I saw the father he was in an acute state of stress, which suggested that he decompensated when stressed. Without either myself, or the unrepresented mother, raising alternatives the judge accepted the proposition made by the QC.

A final aspect learned through this experience was that, even though I had good quality contemporaneous notes, I wished that I had a tape recording of what the father actually said because it was argued that my notes misrepresented what the father had been trying to say. Subsequently, I have considered setting up taping software to keep a verbal record of what is said to me so that if I am ever in the position of having to argue between what I found and what the person said, I can demonstrate my position. The problem with doing this is that I have to get the record transcribed, which takes time and money.

When this case is examined as a whole, what started off as a seemingly cut and dried situation, ended up with a judgment which in essence said that I was swayed by personal feelings of dislike, put too much weight on other evidence which was found to be faulty, and that I was emotive. Ten years of conscientious report writing for the Family Court, and a number of judgments in which I have been found to approach the task with objectivity and caution, were potentially nullified in one trial. The irony in this case was that it was not even one in which I saw the problem coming.

It is easy to personalise a bad court experience. Many skilled practitioners remain traumatised from such experiences. My advice is to ensure that you offload the emotions with a trusted colleague or friend after the experience. Once the emotions are addressed, then analyse the experience so that you can learn from your mistakes. Finally, try to see yourself as a piece of evidence, and avoid having your ego invested excessively in the outcomes of a case.

This case example highlights the underlying message of this book. How you set up your position, structure your evidence and prepare for court are of critical importance, but court is like a game and, even if you play the game to the best of your ability, it is not a game you will win every time. Experienced professionals can sometimes have a difficult time in court even if the situation is managed well.

Final Advice

The final comment I would like to make for your contemplation is that the court process is only like a game, it is not actually a game. The courts are one of the cornerstones of our society and should be treated with the utmost respect. At the risk of playing semantics, you play the game of court; you do not play games with the court or the judge. The quickest way to have your evidence discounted is to present information that is not true, or to take a position other than that of assisting the court. After reading this book, I hope that you will now play a better game, giving due respect to the dignity and importance of the legal system.

Key Points

- Giving evidence is a skill that can be learned.

- Asking lawyers, reading judgments, and having a colleague observe your performance are all means of getting some feedback on your efforts.

- Reflecting on the questions asked during cross-examination gives you an indication of what the lawyers did not understand about your report.

- Reading the literature about giving evidence in court is helpful. However, be selective as some literature can heighten anxieties.

- Do not try to outsmart the lawyers or barristers by focussing on their ploys. The best witness is aware of what a lawyer may be doing, but they stay focussed on giving facts and opinions from their investigations.

- Mistakes may be made, and evidence can go wrong. Try to maintain a position that you are a source of information, rather than allow your ego to be dented.

- Play the game of court, do not play games with the court!

Appendix -
Judge Wisbey -
Draft Paper (2002)

It was with appreciation to Judge Wisbey that I included a copy of his draft paper on the expert witness and presenting expert evidence. Judge Wisbey of the District Court of Western Australia consented to this paper being included in "A reliable witness: how to give credible mental health evidence in court" (2004). I have reproduced the paper in this book, which is a revised and retitled edition of "A reliable witness".

This paper is of considerable assistance to all professionals, not just those who are psychologists, as it outlines what judges, and the law, require of expert witnesses.

THE EXPERT WITNESS &

PRESENTING EXPERT EVIDENCE

What Is Expert Evidence?

In any trial, opinion evidence (that is the opinion of a witness as to the facts) is generally inadmissible. It is for the trial judge to draw all necessary inferences or conclusions from the evidence presented.

The difference between direct evidence of fact, and opinion evidence, correlates with that between lay witnesses and expert witnesses. Lay witnesses give direct evidence of what they have perceived with their senses, but are not permitted to express opinions; that is to express a concluded view based upon perception. Generally opinion evidence cannot be given by lay witnesses.

Opinions by experts are an exception to the general rule to which I have referred. Expert evidence "is admissible whenever the subject matter of the enquiry is such that inexperienced persons are unlikely to prove capable of forming a correct judgment upon it without such assistance, in other words, when it so far partakes of the nature of a science as to require a course of previous habit, or study, in order to the attainment of a knowledge of it".

In the psychological context it may be evidence of fact (the fact that the practitioner is able to demonstrate by appropriate testing that a person has certain intellectual disadvantages or that the testing reveals indicia of a recognisable psychological condition). The psychologist then draws inferences from the objective facts disclosed by psychological testing, and expresses an opinion which is able to be drawn because of that person's expertise or training.

There are three conditions that must be fulfilled before evidence can be received as expert evidence:

1. The person giving the evidence must demonstrate that he or she has the necessary qualifications to speak about matters the subject of the evidence. A witness cannot qualify as an expert unless his or her profession, habit, or a course of study or experience gives him or her a greater capacity of judging the issue than is possessed by other people. Once he or she has demonstrated the necessary qualifications, then he or she is able to offer opinion evidence (notwithstanding that in some cases it may be that the capacity is somewhat at variance with the qualifications).

2. The qualifications or expertise must relate to a matter which is capable of being the subject of expertise – that is of training and/or experience placing the person possessing it in a position to form an educated opinion on the matter not capable of being formed by persons generally. There is no scope for expert evidence in a situation where an unqualified person is capable of forming a valid opinion on the subject.

3. No expert is entitled to deal with a question, the answer to which ultimately depends upon the application of a legal standard, although this comment is easy to make but not so easy to apply.

Psychological Evidence Specifically

A psychologist in a personal injury case or a criminal proceeding can give evidence that he or she carried out an examination or testing of a person, and that the testing did or did not reveal any abnormality in the person tested. He or she cannot express an opinion that the tested person is genuine or malingering. The opinion must not extend to usurping the function of the trial judge in reaching the ultimate conclusion as to whether the person is truthful. That opinion is not admissible as the court is well able and required to draw the appropriate conclusion from the evidence presented.

The Need To Identify The Basis Of The Opinion

The psychological evidence, to be of value, must indicate the base testing information forming the foundation for the ultimate conclusion, and that conclusion must be based as far as possible on objective fact.

In order to facilitate a proper appreciation of the opinion, and a sound evaluation of that opinion and its validity, it is essential the facts upon which the opinion is based are clearly identified. This then enables the application of commonsense and logic to be used to determine the validity of the opinion. The application of forensic logic should generally provide the answer.

It is important to indicate clearly in any report or in evidence, that part of the report or evidence that is based on ascertained fact, and that which is inferential (i.e. conclusions drawn from objective fact).

Evidential rules require that the facts upon which an expert opinion is based be established by admissible evidence. Consequently if an opinion is formed as to the nature and extent of a psychological condition, based in part upon the acceptance of material from another source, that material must also be proved by evidence.

Experience demonstrates that if, when preparing a report, the expert carefully identifies any condition precedent to the conclusions he or she has reached, it may provide an understanding of how and why other experts have taken a different view. Consequently it facilitates dialogue between "opposing" experts and may contribute to an amicable and speedy compromise or resolution of the disputed issue. It also identifies the foundation facts, with the result that agreement may be reached as to those facts, and demonstrate that the forensic controversy is illusionary.

It is important to indicate the extent to which the conclusions reached are based on other material and/or an acceptance of the findings or conclusions of others.

The identification of an assumption of fact that might not be common to the expert contestants, may result in considerable reduction in the time taken up during evidence, and is clearly beneficial to all parties.

It is important that if and when a contrary view has been expressed, one addresses that view, identifying whether the difference is explicable by a difference of objective fact assumption, or is an inferential difference from the established facts.

The Proper Role Of The Expert Witness

It is essential that the expert remain impartial to the cause, and appreciate that his or her obligation is to the truth (the court) rather than the party who has engaged them. The obligation is to present objective evidence.

In an article in the University of Chicago Law Review, the author noted that at the American Trial Bar expert witnesses had come to be known as saxophones, the idea being that the lawyer played the tune, manipulating the expert as though the expert were a musical instrument on which the lawyer sounded the desired notes.

In speaking about the tendency of experts to become partisan, it is important not to lose sight of the fact that a conflict in expert view, reflecting genuine differences of opinion based upon the then state of the psychological science, and perhaps reflecting the patient's presentation, is an important part of the adversarial system.

It is important that the expert avoid adopting the role of a trailblazer for untried or dubious theories. If the expert wishes to be adventurous (and perhaps that shouldn't be discouraged) it is important that he or she enunciates clearly the novelty of the view, and identifies any opposing views.

The Necessity To Keep An Open Mind

A criticism of the adversarial system is that it discourages experts adopting a conciliatory approach thus narrowing areas of disagreement. The system also discourages experts from making concessions, once reports have been exchanged. There are very few of us who are not driven by ego, and the more experienced and senior we become in our particular area of expertise, the more difficult it becomes to recognise and compensate therefore.

Once an expert has given evidence-in-chief, he or she is reluctant during cross-examination to receive and accommodate contrary views concerned that it may be seen as a sign of weakness, or a lack of capacity. It is for that reason that an informal exchange of views prior to a trial is of assistance. If the expert is prepared to make himself available to address the concerns of each side prior to any hearing, there is a real possibility for accommodation of views.

There are often occasions when an expert, confronted during his or her evidence with material of which he or she was not previously aware, will not be prepared to acknowledge that it has any relevance or impact on his or her opinion. It is important that you are prepared to accommodate new material and to acknowledge that it impacts upon your opinion if that is the case. A witness should not be frightened to indicate to the trial judge that he or she would need time to reflect on the new material before indicating whether or not it affects the opinion that has been expressed.

Key Points

When preparing a report or giving evidence it is important that an expert:

- Set out fully the history provided by the client.

- Identify with particularity the base material (factual assumptions) upon which the ultimate conclusion is founded.

- Be as concise and precise as the subject permits.

- Be as frank, objective and non-controversial as is possible consistent with professional obligation.

- Does not reject an opposing view out of hand, but is prepared to consider and evaluate it with a view to distinguishing or accommodating it.

- Be conscious of the limits of his or her area of expertise and ensures that the evidence is contained by it.

- Be mindful of the fact that his or her obligation is to assist the tribunal of fact and not to usurp its task of determining the credibility of the litigant.

Index

Reference List and Further Reading

Ackerman, M. (2006). Clinician's guide to child custody evaluations (3rd ed.). New York: John Wiley.

Ackerman, M. (1999). Essentials of forensic psychological assessment. New York: John Wiley and Sons.

Australian Government Solicitors (2003, rev. reprint). Australia's constitution. Canberra: AGS.

Australian Psychological Society Ltd (APS). (2007). Code of ethics. Carlton, Vic: APS.

Babitsky, S. and Mangraviti, J.J. (2002). Writing and defending your expert report. Maine: SEAK Inc.

Babitsky, S. and Mangraviti, J.J. (2003). Cross examination: the comprehensive guide for experts. Maine: SEAK Inc.

Brodksy, S. (1991). Testifying in court. Washington: APA.

Byrne, D. (1986). Cross on evidence. Sydney: Butterworths.

Champagne, A., Shuman, D. & Whitaker, E. (1992). "Expert witnesses in the courts: an empirical examination". Judicature, 76, 5-10.
Cohen, E. (1995). The law and the diving professional. Santa Ana, California: PADI.

Davidson, G. (2002). "Dealing with subpoenas". InPsych, 24(5), 31.
Dvoskin, J.A. & Guy, L.S. (2008). "On being an expert witness: it's not about you". Psychiatry, Psychology and Law, 15 (2), 202-212.

Faust, D. & Ziskin, J. (1988). "The expert witness in psychology and psychiatry". Science, 241, 31-35.
Freckelton, I.R., Reddy, P. & Selby, H. (1999). Australian judicial perspectives on expert evidence: An empirical study. Carlton, Australia: Australian Institute of Judicial Administration Inc.

Garb, H. (1992). "The trained psychologist as expert witness". Clinical Psychology Review, 12, 451-467.
Gaughwin, P.C. (2004). "Beyond the noise and smoke: some challenges for the mental health professionals entering the forensic area". ANZPPL, 11 (1), 44-49.
Gould, J.W. (2006). Conducting scientifically crafted child custody evaluations (2nd ed.). Florida: Professional Resources.

Kapardis, A. (1998). "Psychology and law in Australia: an overview". Law In Context, 16, 106-117.
Kane (1999). "Essentials of Malingering assessment". Essentials of forensic assessment, Ackerman M.J. (ed.). 78

McBride, N. & Tunnecliffe, M. (2001). Risky Practices.
    Perth: Bayside Books.
McCann, J.T. & Dyer, F.J. (1996). Forensic assessment with
    the Millon Inventories. New York: Guilford Press.
McNamara, B. (1999). How Australia is governed:
    a simple guide to Australia's system of
    parliamentary democracy. Fyshwick, ACT: CanPrint
    Communications.
Melton, G., Petrila, J., Poythress, N.G., & Slobogin, C.
    (1987). Psychological evaluations for the courts (3 ed.).
    New York: Guilford Press.

Royal Australian and New Zealand College of
    Psychiatrists (RANZCP). (2003). Ethical and practice
    guidelines #9: Ethical guidelines for independent
    medical examinations and report preparation.

Sattler, J. (1998). Clinical and forensic interviewing of
    children and families. San Diego: Jerome Sattler
    Publishing.
Selby, H. & Blank, G. (2004). Winning advocacy.
    Melbourne: Oxford Uni Press
Stevens, B.A. (2008). Crossfire!: skills for psychologists
    giving expert evidence in court. Queensland:
    Academic Press.

McBride, N. & Tunnecliffe, M. (2001). Risky Practices.
    Perth: Bayside Books.

Watts, P.S. (2008). Shared care or divided lives?: what's
    best for children when parents separate. Perth: Ogilvie
    Publishing.
Watts, P.S. (2004). A reliable witness: how to give credible
    mental health evidence in Court. Perth: Ogilvie
    Publishing.

Wetter, M. & Corrigan, S. (1995). "Providing information to clients about psychological tests: a questionnaire of attorneys' and law students' attitudes". Professional Psychology: Research and Practice, 26, 474-477.

White, J., Day, A., & Hackett, L. (2007). Writing reports for court. Queensland: Academic Press.

Ziskin, J. & Faust, D. (1995). Coping with psychiatric and psychological testimony (5th ed.). Los Angeles: Law & Psychology Press.

CASES
Price v R (1981) TasR 306 CCA
R v Whitbread (1995) 78 ACrimR 452
Steffen v Ruban (1966) 84 WN(Pt.1)(NSW) 264

LEGISLATION
Family Law Rules 2004 (Cwlth)
Family Law Amendment (Shared Parental Responsibility) Act 2006 (Cwlth)
Freedom of Information Act 1982 (Cwlth)
Privacy Act 1988 (Cwlth)

About the Author

Dr Phil Watts is a well-known Western Australian clinical and forensic psychologist and is a past president of the WA branch of the APS forensic college. After completing a Master's degree in Clinical Psychology in 1989 (and a Doctor of Philosophy in 1994), he worked for the Department of Community Development and Ministry of Justice before commencing a private practice in 1994. He runs a mixed practice involving forensic assessment and clinical treatment of families, adults and children.

A significant aspect of his practice includes running training programmes for various professions. Of particular note are his national tours to provide training to health professionals (six tours around Australia since 2003) on how to give evidence in court, report writing for court, in the witness box skills training, assessing complex families for court, understanding internet pornography, and assessment of risk in clinical practice.

With over 500 appointments as court expert in the Family Court, and over 600 reports for other courts, he is highly experienced in psychological assessment for court. He has given evidence in numerous trials in the Children's, Family, District, and Supreme Courts. An interesting peculiarity is that he actually enjoys giving evidence in court!

www.ingramcontent.com/pod-product-compliance
Lightning Source LLC
Chambersburg PA
CBHW071208210326
41597CB00016B/1724

* 9 7 8 0 9 7 5 6 0 4 2 2 9 *